Lost Traditions

OBSOLETE OCCUPATIONS
and
FORGOTTEN PASTIMES

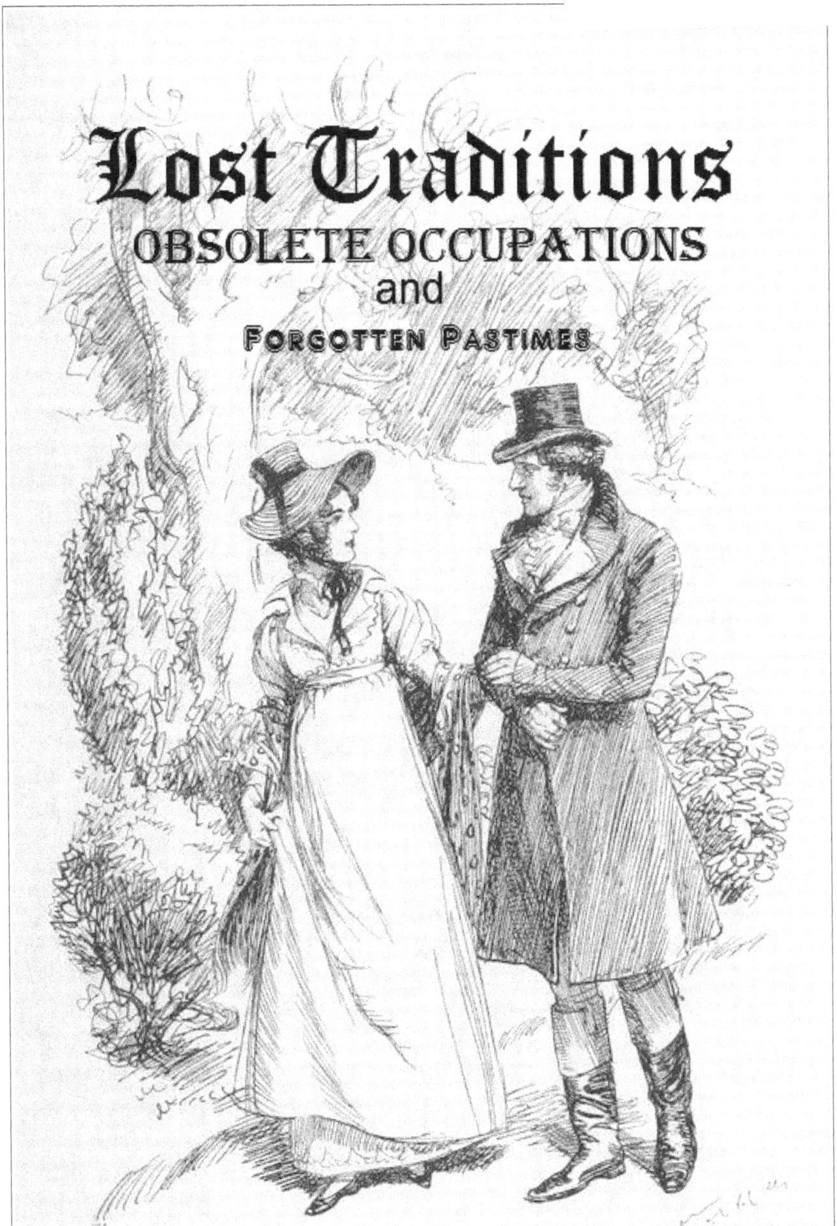

John Louis Sublett

LOST TRADITIONS

Obsolete Occupations
and
FORGOTTEN PASTIMES

Tradition: *An inherited, established, or customary pattern of thought, action, or behavior (as a religious practice or social custom). The handing down of information, beliefs, and customs by word of mouth or by example from one generation to another without written instruction. Cultural continuity in social attitudes, customs, and institutions. Characteristic manner, method, or style.*

Table of Contents

A fiddler on the roof. Sounds crazy, no? But in our little village of Anatevka, every one of us is a fiddler on the roof trying to scratch out a pleasant, simple tune without breaking his neck. It isn't easy. You may ask, why do we stay here if it's so dangerous? We stay because Anatevka is our home. And how do we keep our balance? That, I can tell you in one word:

Tradition!

Because of our traditions, we have kept our balance for many, many years. Here in Anatevka, we have traditions for everything: how to eat, how to sleep, how to wear clothes. For instance, we always keep our heads covered, and always wear a little prayer-shawl. This shows our constant devotion to God. You may ask, how did this tradition start? I'll tell you. I don't know. But it's a tradition. And because of our traditions, every one of us knows who he is, and what God expects him to do.

Traditions, traditions. Without our traditions, our lives would be as shaky as... as... as a fiddler on the roof!

Courtships & Weddings

1. **RIBBONS** - Saving the ribbons from the bridal shower gifts to make a mock bouquet to be used at the wedding rehearsal.

2. **BACHELORS' DAY** - According to an old Irish legend, or possibly history, St Bridget struck a deal with St Patrick to allow women to propose to men – and not just the other way around – every 4 years. This is believed to have been introduced to balance the traditional roles of men and women in a similar way to how Leap Day balances the calendar. In some places, Leap Day has been known as "Bachelors' Day" for the same reason. A man was expected to pay a penalty, such as a gown or money, if he refused a marriage proposal from a woman on Leap Day. In many European countries, especially in the upper classes of society, tradition dictates that any man who refuses a woman's proposal on February 29 has to buy her 12 pairs of gloves. The intention is that the woman can wear the gloves to hide the embarrassment of not having an engagement ring. During the middle ages there were laws governing this tradition.

3. **POLTERABEND** - is a German pre-wedding tradition where friends and family come together for an informal party. While that may not seem

odd, what they do at these parties certainly is. They break dishes, flowerpots, tiles, toilets, pretty much anything except glasses or mirrors. To symbolize working together through future difficulties, the bride and groom must clean everything up. Due to the need to replace all the broken goods, I suspect that German sellers of housewares are quite fond of this custom.

4. **BLACKENING THE BRIDE** - To prepare for their marriage, Scottish brides-to-be must go through a very foul pre-wedding ritual. Friends of the bride take her by surprise and cover her with eggs, spoiled milk, feathers, pretty much anything disgusting. The blackened bride is then paraded around town. The purpose of this custom is to prepare the bride for marriage because after going through that, any marital problems will seem like nothing.

5. **MEET THE PARENTS** - custom that a boy would first meet a girl's parents before taking her out

6. **BUNDLING** - Northern US courtship traditions were rather surprising. Many would engage in a practice called "bundling." Believed to be a Dutch tradition, the man and woman would be tucked into bed together, sometimes dressed and sometimes only partially clothed. This was meant to build intimacy between the potential

couple without being, um, intimate. As you may have guessed this resulted in more than its fair share of, shall we call them, "early births" in the marriages. Go figure.

7. **COURTING** - Southern US courtship traditions more closely resembled our current dating habits, albeit a more controlled version. A typical southern courtship consisted of visits from the suitor for a pleasant evening conversing on the porch or in the parlor all while under the watchful eye of a chaperone.

8. **PROPOSAL REFUSAL** - In the southern US it was not uncommon, and was actually considered good form for women to refuse her suitor's proposals not just once, but at least twice if not more before accepting his offer of marriage. That's gotta be rough. Poor fellas!

9. **WHITE WEDDING GOWNS**? No way. Brown or dove grey silk bridal gowns were the colors of choice once upon a time. The bridesmaids were the ones who wore white.

10. **DOWRIES** - the money, goods, or estate that a woman brings to her husband or his family in marriage. Most common in cultures that are strongly patrilineal and that expect women to reside with or near their husband's family.

John Louis Sublett

Stores & Shopping

1. **GREEN AND PLAID STAMPS** - S&H Green Stamps were trading stamps popular in the U.S. from the 1930s to the 1980s. They were distributed as part of a rewards program operated by the Sperry & Hutchinson Co. (S&H), founded in 1896. During the 1960s, the rewards catalog printed by the company was the largest publication in the U.S. and the company issued three times as many stamps as the U.S. Postal Service. Customers would receive stamps at the checkout counter of supermarkets, department stores, and gasoline stations among other retailers, which could be redeemed for products in the catalog. The Plaid Stamp program was run by A & P supermarkets.

2. **THE 'BLUE LAW'** - Stores were always closed on Sundays – people used to have Sunday as a day to visit family (a blue law is a type of law designed to restrict or ban some or all Sunday shopping for religious standards, particularly the observance of a day of worship or rest.)

3. **NICKEL PICKLE** - The nickel for a pickle in the big wooden barrel with all the pickle juice

4. **VIDEO STORES** - Who needs a video store

when you've got Netflix, RedBox, iTunes, Hulu, Amazon Prime

5. **TRAVEL AGENTS** - the creation of websites like Kayak, Orbitz, Travelocity, and Priceline, which made it easy to find their our fares and easily book their our flights have changed the travel industry in dramatic ways. The days of recruiting a travel agent to book flights, find hotels, and organize tours are on their way out, already gone for many.

6. **AUTOMATS** - An automat is a fast food restaurant where simple foods and drink are served by coin-operated and bill-operated vending machines. Horn & Hardart were the big company in this business starting around 1912 in NYC

7. **MOM AND POP STORES** - There's just something so wonderful about small-town, family owned stores isn't there? Whether it's a small grocery store, a clothing store, a book store, a café, or a restaurant, they just feel like home. They have personality. What's more awesome than having coffee with a friend at a small-town café? What stirs the imagination like spending hours reading in a small-town book store? They are each unique unto themselves, whereas the large chain stores and restaurants are impersonal and are basically just clones of each other.

8. **SODA JERKS**

John Louis Sublett

Holidays

THANKSGIVING MASKERS (Ragamuffin parades) (Seems to have been mainly an east coast tradition) ragamuffins and their colorful antics had been born in New York City's Brooklyn neighborhoods where European families had settled, and from which the observation would branch out only to nearby enclaves

Before Halloween became the holiday it now is in the United States, children would dress up in masks on the final Thursday in November and go door to door for treats (think: fruit!), or scramble for pennies. The tradition was known as Thanksgiving Masking. Thanksgiving 'masking', as it was often called, stemmed from a satirical perversion of destitution and the ancient tradition of mumming, where men in costumes floated from door to door, asking for food and money, often in exchange for music. In the 19th century, makeshift Thanksgiving parades -- fantasticals -- featured New Yorkers marching through the street in garish costume.
an old custom from over a hundred years ago, especially popular among poor New York City children, might scare the stuffing out of a Thanksgiving dinner party today. Imagine opening your home to invited guests, only to find a group of children in wretched and unsettling disguises, disfigured masks and poverty-inspired costumes, knocking at your door and begging for sweets

LEAP DAY (BACHELORS DAY) – February 29th happens once every four years - According to an old Irish legend, or possibly history, St. Bridget struck a deal with St. Patrick to allow women to propose to men – and not just the other way around – every 4 years. This is believed to have been introduced to balance the traditional roles of men and women in a similar way to how Leap Day balances the calendar.

In some places, Leap Day has been known as "Bachelors' Day" for the same reason. A man was expected to pay a penalty, such as a gown or money, if he refused a marriage proposal from a woman on Leap Day. In many European countries, especially in the upper classes of society, tradition dictates that any man who refuses a woman's proposal on February 29 has to buy her 12 pairs of gloves. The intention is that the woman can wear the gloves to hide the embarrassment of not having an engagement ring. During the middle ages there were laws governing this tradition.

ROASTING CHESTNUTS - Roasting chestnuts dates back centuries, when people turned up the heat on these nuts for more than just festive fare. Chestnuts became a staple in the mountainous regions around the Mediterranean Sea thousands of years ago, in part because most cereal grains couldn't grow in these areas. These flavorful nuts can supply a feast of nutrients: They are low in fat, high in fiber , and packed with minerals

DRIVE AROUND LOOKING AT CHRISTMAS

LIGHTS - I don't mean searching "Christmas lights" on YouTube, I mean making a night of getting in the car, getting hot cocoa and admiring all of the work that people have put into their homes. There are some spectacular displays, and probably in your own neighborhood if you just take the time to find them.

MAIL DELIVERY - more than one mail delivery during the holidays

BOBBING FOR APPLES - Each member of the party is given an apple, from which a small piece has been cut, and into which a fortune written on a slip of paper has been inserted. The apples are thrown into a large tub of water and the company invited to duck their heads and retrieve an apple with their mouths. Upon doing so, they draw out the slip of paper and read their fortune.

ADVENT CALENDARS - An advent calendar is a card or poster with twenty-four small doors, one to be opened each day from December 1 until Christmas Eve. Each door conceals a picture. This popular tradition arose in Germany in the late 1800s and soon spread throughout Europe and North America. Originally, the images in Advent calendars were derived from the Hebrew Bible. Considered a fun way of counting down the days until Christmas, many Advent calendars today have no religious content. Now, alongside traditional Advent calendars depicting angels and biblical figures are those whose doors open to display teddy bears, pieces of chocolate, or photos of pop stars.

CUT DOWN YOUR OWN TREE – a line from a famous Christmas movie says it well - "most people are satisfied with scrawny, dead, over priced trees that have no special meaning"

CHRISTMAS PUDDING (Plum Pudding) , The plum pudding's association with Christmas takes us back to medieval England and the Roman Catholic Church's decree that the 'pudding should be made on the twenty-fifth Sunday after Trinity, that it be prepared with thirteen ingredients to represent Christ and the twelve apostles, and that every family member stir it in turn from east to west to honor the Magi and their supposed journey in that direction.' It is customary, before sending it to the table, to make a little hole in the top and fill it with brandy, then light it, and serve it in a blaze. An important addition to the mixture was a silver coin, a thimble, and a ring. He who is served the coin finds luck, he who retrieves the thimble brings himself prosperity, and he who comes up with the ring hastens a wedding in his family.

TWELFTH NIGHT CAKE - it was not a

Christmas cake, but a Twelfth Night Cake. The Twelfth night is on the 5th of January, and has been for centuries the traditional last day of the Christmas season.. It was a time for having a great feast, and the cake was an essential part of the festivities. This was slightly different in different countries, and also at different social levels. In the GREAT HOUSES, into the cake was baked a dried Bean and a Pea. one in one half and the other in the other half. The cake was decorated with sugar and ornamentation. As the visitors arrived, they were given a piece of the cake, ladies from the left, gentlemen from the right side. Whoever got the bean became King of the Revels for the night, and everyone had to do as he said. The lady was his Queen for the evening. In smaller homes, the cake was a simple fruit cake, with a bean in it, which was given to guests during the twelve days of Christmas. Whoever got the bean was supposed to be a kind of guardian angel for that family for the year, so it was an important task, and usually, it was arranged that a senior member of the family would get the bean! This was observed until recently in Poland in fact. In Britain the cake was baked as part of the refreshments offered to the priest and his entourage who would visit on the feast of the Epiphany, January 6th, to bless each house in the parish. this custom died out after the Reformation in the late 16th century.. In

Mallorca, the main island of the Spanish Balearics Islands, they have a similar custom which takes place at Easter. The festive cake in Britain was revived at the end of the 17th century, and became very much part of the Twelfth night partying again. It is recorded In royal households, that the cakes became extravagantly large, and the guests divided into two sides could have a battle with models on the cake! One battle was a sea battle, and there were miniature water canons on the cake which really worked!

'CALLING' ON NEW YEARS DAY - Instead of spending New Year's Day nursing a hangover, 19th century New York gentlemen went 'calling' - visiting the homes of ladies with whom they were acquainted. There they had a bit of food and drink, dropped off a calling card, and wished their host a Happy New Year before moving on to the next house. Men competed to visit the most ladies; women vied to get the most calling cards. The women - wives, mothers, sisters, aunts, cousins, and their staffs - spent days preparing for the visits, fixing themselves up and laying out vast spreads of food and spirits upon tables and sidebars. It wasn't unusual for a group of men to visit sixty or seventy women from morning to night.

MAKE YOUR OWN DECORATIONS

STRINGING POPCORN for the Christmas tree - this tradition started in Europe. The trees were decorated outside, to feed the birds, they would string berries and nuts as well as popcorn. A Christmas tree was decorated just to feed the wildlife that could not get any food because of the snow.

TINSEL - a Christmas tree decoration that mimics icicles. Originally tinsel was made of silver and hung like garland on a tree. Usually only wealthy people could afford to hang tinsel on their tree. Manufacturers started making tinsel out of other metals, but it wasn't until the 1950's that tinsel caught on. In the 1950's, manufacturers made plastic tinsel for Christmas decorations. The tinsel was affordable so everyone could use it.

BANGING POTS AND PANS ON NEW YEARS EVE - The idea of making deafening noise is to drive away the evil spirits who flocked to the living at this climactic season with a great wailing of horns and shouts and beating of drums. This is why at the stroke of midnight we hear the deafening cacophony of sirens, car horns, boat whistles, party horns, church bells, drums, pots and pans.

THE GIVING OF FRUITCAKES - One of the main reasons fruitcakes were given as gifts in early times is that the ingredients combined in such a way as to greatly reduce the spoiling of this food. This was a huge advantage when the average family had very little control over their food supply, and allowed people to travel longer distances since they could carry a food supply with them that would not spoil.

RAVELETTE BALLS (Surprise Balls) - They were basically balls that you unravel, and as you "unraveled" the ball you'd find treats and little presents in each layer. They were given at different holidays

TWELVE DAYS OF CHRISTMAS – ending with the celebration of 'The Twelfth Night' - what happened to the Twelve Days of Christmas? Starting at sunset on December 25th and going through sunset on January 6th seems like a much more fun idea than one day a year. The Twelve Days of Christmas are the festive days beginning Christmas Day (25 December). This period is also known as Christmastide and Twelvetide. The Twelfth Night of Christmas is always on the evening of 5 January, but the Twelfth Day can either precede or follow the Twelfth Night according to which Christian tradition is followed. Twelfth Night is followed by the Feast of the Epiphany on 6 January. In some traditions, the first day of Epiphany (6 January) and the twelfth day of Christmas overlap. This is the Church festival of Ephiphany. The traditional day when Christians celebrate the arrival of the Magi or Three Kings in Bethlehem. It used to be the time when people exchanged their Christmas gifts. The feast was marked, as were all the old feasts, by some kind of religious observance. A visit to the church, a service or some kind, and then a folk observance which was tightly wrapped up as part of the Church activities. As we have seen, Twelve Day (the day following Twelfth Night) entailed the blessing of the home, and in some countries is still observed. But after the Reformation, these customs of the Church were banned by the Puritans, and fell into disuse. Without its religious overtones, Twelfth Night became a time of mischief and over indulgence. By 1870, Britain's Queen Victoria announced that she felt it was inappropriate to hold such an unchristian festival, and Twelfth Night was banned as a feast-day.

TELLING GHOST STORIES AT CHRISTMAS - Imagine your whole family gathered around the blazing fire on Christmas Eve, with snow falling outside and hot drinks all around, and Grandpa starts to tell a blood-curdling tale of murder and monsters. Strange as this might sound, telling ghost stories used to be a very common Christmas tradition. The iconic British Christmas story, A Christmas Carol by Charles Dickens, was originally subtitled A Ghost Story of Christmas.

The Victorians certainly enjoyed this tradition. In 1891 English writer Jerome K. Jerome noted, "Whenever five or six English-speaking people meet round a fire on Christmas Eve, they start telling each other ghost stories. Nothing satisfies us on Christmas Eve but to hear each other tell authentic anecdotes about specters." Perhaps subsequent generations trying to weed out some of Christmas's pagan roots thought that ghost stories smacked too much of ancient winter solstice rituals and heathen symbolism. These supernatural elements are now relegated to Halloween, but perhaps it would not be amiss to relive a Victorian Christmas by lighting candles and reading A Christmas Carol aloud to the family-ghoulish sound effects and all.(One verse of Andy Williams' classic Christmas song "It's the Most Wonderful Time of the Year," for instance, clearly says, "There'll be scary ghost stories and tales of the glories of Christmases long, long ago.") The most obvious example of how Victorian ghost stories have persisted to some degree in modern Christmas celebrations, however, is of course Charles Dickens' own "ghostly little story" (as he calls it in the introduction) "A Christmas Carol."In the last few decades, though, perhaps one of the most interesting Victorian Christmas traditions has been almost completely lost from memory."Whenever five or six English-speaking people meet round a fire on Christmas Eve, they start telling each other ghost stories," wrote British humorist Jerome K. Jerome as part of his introduction to an anthology of Christmas ghost stories titled "Told After Supper" in 1891. "Nothing satisfies us on Christmas Eve but to hear each other tell authentic anecdotes about specters."The practice of gathering around the fire on Christmas Eve to tell ghost stories was as much a part of Christmas for the Victorian English as Santa Claus is for us.

CHRISTMAS CAROLING - St. Francis of Assisi was instrumental in making the Christmas celebration one for the people instead of just for the clergy. He created large nativity scenes outside of his church and translated many of the Christmas carols from Latin into languages spoken by the average person and encouraged them to sing these songs to express their joy during the Christmas season. This practice of singing Christmas songs outside of the Church near the nativity scenes spread throughout Europe and it was a natural next step for these Christmas Carolers to start walking through the neighborhoods around the churches sharing their festive songs. Caroling started to decline in popularity as people were able to hear and play the same songs on the radio and eventually on their own record players

MAY DAY – this forgotten holiday was celebrated by some early European settlers of the American continent. In some parts of the United States, May Baskets are made. These are small baskets usually filled with flowers or treats and left at someone's doorstep. The giver rings the bell and runs away. The person receiving the basket tries to catch the fleeing giver; if caught, a kiss is exchanged. During the Cold War, May Day celebrations fell out of favor due to its association with the USSR. This holiday also included dancing around a maypole. The origin of May Day is indissolubly bound up with the struggle for the shorter workday – a demand of major political significance for the working class. This struggle is manifest almost from the beginning of the factory system in the United States. Although the demand for higher wages appears to be the most prevalent cause of the early strikes in this country, the question of shorter hours and the right to organize were always kept in the foreground when workers formulated their demands against the bosses and the government. As exploitation was becoming intensified and workers were feeling more and more the strain of inhumanly long working hours, the demand for an appreciable reduction of hours became more pronounced. Already at the opening of the 19th century workers in the United States made known their grievances against working from "sunrise to sunset," the then prevailing workday. Fourteen, sixteen and even eighteen hours a day were not uncommon. During the conspiracy trial against the leaders of striking cordwainers in 1806, it was brought out that the workers were employed as long as nineteen and twenty hours a day.

ALUMINUM CHRISTMAS TREES - During the late '50s, production of $25 Christmas trees with foil branches and aluminum needles soared as homeowners loved the efficiency of a tree with no needles to sweep and baby boomers with visions of a far-out rocket-powered future in their heads could stare at the gleaming metallic wonder in their living rooms.

Trees were pink, blue, silver or whatever color the color-wheel projector below shone on them. The best part was that the tree, the ornaments, the stand and all the other accessories could be placed in one box and packed away tidily until the next holiday season.

Unfortunately, pop art's holiday answer to the pink flamingo was imperiled when Charles Schultz's A Charlie Brown Christmas mocked gaudy pink aluminum trees as hollow, soulless totems to commercialism and made a tattered natural tree branch into a national folk hero and the embodiment of Christmas Spirit, it signaled disaster for aluminum tree sales.

HIGH-WATTAGE HOLIDAY LIGHTS - Go out shopping for Christmas lights this season and you'll come across mini lights, LED lights, C7

big-bulb lights and C9 bigger-bulb lights.
What you won't find is grandma and grandpa's
C6 lights, with good reason. Those C6 bulbs
were bright, lovely and festive, but insanely hot.
They "got hot enough to set fire to anything
combustible if left in contact long enough." When
the paint chipped off of these bulbs, as it tended
to do frequently, they let loose a glaring white
light that not only overwhelmed the color of the
rest of the bulbs, but would singed anything it
came into contact with. These bulbs eventually
gave way to the cooler-burning C7 bulbs that
looked just as lovely, but also burned fairly hot.
Manufacturers still advise turning them on their
bases so their bulbs don't come in contact with a
tree's needles and set it ablaze. The large C9
lights are just bad news for indoor use altogether
and best kept outside.

All of these varieties started to take a backseat
during the 1970's, when smaller, cooler and
more energy-efficient mini lights came into
vogue. They're still a pain to fix if a bulb goes out
in a strand, but a 50-foot string costs just $1.38
to operate for 300 hours, compared with $8 for a
C7 strand of the same size, according to
Consumer Reports. The biggest threat to the big,
hot bulbs, however, is LED bulbs.

THE KISSING BOUGH - Kissing under the
mistletoe is now all that remains of the
customary "holy bough", a ball woven from ash,

willow or hazel twigs with a figure of the Christ-child in the center. This "Sacramental" was blessed by a priest and hung inside the threshold of a house, symbolizing goodwill and peace to all visitors. The custom goes back to Viking times, when mistletoe – considered sacred by the Druids – was hung outside Viking homes as a sign of welcome to strangers. Ribbons, candles, gilded nuts and small apples or dried fruit were often hung from the bough in later years, not without a certain "keeping up with the Joneses" element as neighbors vied with one another for the best-decorated bough. However, this and many other Christmas customs fell from favor in the Puritan era, when they were seen as having heathen associations and the Christ child figure denounced as an effigy. By the time the custom was remembered and revived by the Victorians, it had become the simpler "kissing bough" – a bunch of mistletoe and other evergreens hung overhead, with those caught standing underneath obliged to reward their captor with a kiss.

Sports

THE SUNDAY BASEBALL DOUBLEHEADER - In 1959, at least one league played a quarter of their games as classic doubleheaders, which declined to 10% in 1979 and further to the point that there were eight years between the last two scheduled official doubleheaders. Reasons for the decline include clubs' desire to maximize revenue, longer duration of games, five day pitching rotation as opposed to four day rotation, time management of relievers and catchers, and lack of consensus among the players.

FOOTBALL BOWL GAMES - Before World War II, there were only five bowls: the Rose, Sugar, Orange, Cotton and Sun. But in the post-war years, sports promoters and civic leaders banked on America's passion for sports, and a number of new bowls were created. The Bluebonnet Bowl and the College All-Star game are among the traditions that once had their place:
There really was a Salad Bowl in Phoenix. Also, the Dixie Bowl in Birmingham, Ala., the Oil Bowl in Houston, the Raisin Bowl in Fresno, Calif., and the Camellia Bowl in Lafayette, La. Tampa's Cigar Bowl lasted a bit longer, from 1946 to 1954. In the 1990 Blockbuster Bowl in Miami.

THE FOUL LINE - Many major league baseball players were superstitious of stepping on the foul line coming on and off the field.

THE BULLPEN CAR - bullpen cars last roamed ballparks nearly 20 years ago, whisking relief pitchers to the mound during games. But once nearly every big league team had a bullpen car; it was typically a tricked-out golf cart with a gigantic replica of the host team's cap as the roof.

KEEPING SCORE – when people buy a program at a baseball park, the vendor gives them a little pencil, most people have no idea what the pencil is for - Consider, first, that keeping score is not just a matter of recording the game. It is, rather, a way of thinking about the game. The score keeper asks, what is happening? Is that an earned run? Did the runner reach first on a fielder's choice, or did he get a hit? Is that a sacrifice, or was the batter bunting for a hit? In order to keep score, you need to make these kinds of decisions. And in order to make these kinds of decisions you need to be closely engaged with the game. You need to pay attention. You need to understand what is going on. You need to have skill. You need to care. But is is a Lost Tradition

NFL COACHES WEARING SUITS

Of all the long-extinct traditions we miss about the NFL, the practice of coaches wearing suits on the sidelines might be our most lamented. It made the game seem more epic, as if these were truly generals commanding men on the field of battle, if generals wore plaid ties and wore fedoras. It classed up the game, made if feel as if it were run by gentlemen, and we were frustrated and confused when the NFL refused 49ers coach Mike Nolan's request last year to wear a suit rather than the traditional (and ridiculous) windbreaker or parka.

KEEPING SCORE AT BOWLING

No longer do people need to learn how to keep score. While some people have no problem making tabulations for each frame, some people do not know how to accurately keep score, since you get bonus points for spares and strikes. Most bowling alleys have computers that do the scoring for you. Now you can concentrate on improving your score and not if you had done your math right.

SPALDEENS

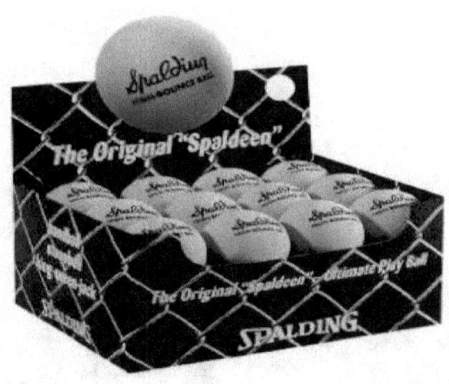

The good old pink, rubber "Spaldeen" Spaldeens were available from 1949 to 1979 to city kids. In urban areas, sparse in grass, Spaldeens became integral to many street games due to their bounciness and light weight. Citing the declining popularity of stickball, Spalding took the ball off the market in 1979, but it returned in 1999 to much fanfare. The retail price in the mid-1960s in Jersey City was 29 cents.

In the documentary New York Street Games, celebrities discuss their memories of games they played as children growing up in New York City. Many of these games involved Spaldeens. At one point, Whoopi Goldberg is talking and rolling a Spaldeen in her hand. When she brings it to her nose and smells it, you can tell by the look on her face that she's reliving memories of happy hours with Spaldeens.

HUNTING CAMPS

With three or more generations occupying the same cabin on the same opening day are becoming lost traditions. Traditionally sporting camps were always "remote", which made them desirable destinations for fishing, hunting, and other types of outdoor recreation. Remote camps are typically rustic wilderness log cabins without such modern utilities as indoor plumbing, electricity or telephone lines; but many have been updated or adjusted to make for a more comfortable stay. Many remote camps use propane gas mantle lanterns for light, wood-burning stoves for heat and cooking, and gravity fed water for flush toilets and showers or bathhouses. Propane refrigerators and stoves replace the need for electric ones, and a generator may be found on site for various camp chores requiring electricity.

THE 'COMPLETE GAME' - by a baseball pitcher is long gone. This change has been brought about by strict adherence to pitch counts as a basis for removing a pitcher, even though he may appear to be pitching well, and new pitching philosophies in general. Many have come to believe that the risk of arm injuries becomes far more prevalent after a pitcher has thrown 100 to 120 pitches in a single game.

PEPPER - Ballplayers (especially visitors) are notorious for getting to the park early and having much time to kill. A pregame staple was players coming down to the field in mid-afternoon for a robust game of "pepper"
One batter, several fielders, 10-15 feet away in a line, making tosses that the batter would hit back at the players, hopefully on one, hard-to-handle hop. Generally, the punishment for booting the ball was to be sent to the end of the line, and farther from his chance to be the batter.
Pepper was the enemy of groundskeepers. The game usually took place behind home plate, beating up the grass. "No Pepper" started appearing in paint on the short wall behind the plate – the area now used for advertising

John Louis Sublett

Birthdays

BIRTHDAY SPANKINGS - there was a tradition of "birthday spankings" where the birthday girl or boy receives the same number of hits as his/her age (plus "one to grow on") during the birthday party. Birthday spankings are administered over the clothes and usually by close friends or family members, and are generally playful swats not meant to cause real pain. The tradition is often seen as a sign of good luck and it is said that it is reminiscent of the way that doctors pat the bottoms of newborn infants to stimulate their bodies into action more quickly.

BIRTHDAY PUNCHES - where the person whose birthday it is being punched a number of times equal to his/her age, often with one additional punch "for luck".

BIRTHDAY CORSAGES FOR GIRLS - A popular tradition of the 1950s and '60s. A young girl might receive a "candy corsage" from her friends on her birthday. Decorated with candy such as lollipops, gum drops, tootsie rolls, bubble gum or lemon drops, such corsages were inexpensive to make and were held together with curly ribbon.

Year	Candy	Meaning
10	Lollipops	Unknown
11	Gumdrops	Unknown
12	Tootsie Rolls	Unknown
13	Bubble Gum	Unknown
14	Dog Biscuits	Puppy Love
15	Lifesavers	Unknown
16	Sugar Cubes	Sweet 16
17	Lemon Drops	Sour 17
18	Cigarettes or Beer Bottle Caps	Coming of Legal Age

Also, in some places where the drinking age was 18 instead of 21, beer bottle caps might have replaced the cigarettes.

Everyday Things

SHOE REPAIR - Over 50,000 shoe repair shops served different American communities in 1922

BAKING BREAD

OPEN A CAR DOOR for a lady

BEDTIME STORIES

THE FAMILY DOCTOR AND HOUSE CALLS

SHOE SHINES - The sad thing is there aren't many places left where you can get your shoes shined. With the exception of a prison unit or a stock exchange, there are few places where this old service can be observed today. It is still true that in high-end hotels, you can put your shoes in a special bag, hang them on your doorknob and in the morning find your shoes have been beautifully polished and left by your door.

WRITING A LETTER TO SOMEONE

BORROWING A BOOK AT THE LIBRARY

TEEN DANCES

HORSE DRAWN VEGETABLE WAGON

THE ICE MAN – he would bring around 300-pound ice blocks, using an ice pick to chip off whatever amount a family needed. He'd carry the ice into the house, where it was stored in a compartment of the icebox to keep the rest ``We loved it when he'd chip the ice block because we got to have the chips."

DIAPER MAN - before Huggies we used a diaper service. They used cloth diapers back then. Soiled ones would be picked up and sent out to be laundered and returned freshly cleaned.

THE RAG MAN

THE FAMILY MEAL

HOME PHOTOGRAPHERS came to customers, often bringing along ponies and goats to pose with children.

UNLOCKED DOORS No one locked their doors

MAKING WINE OUT BACK – the Italian neighbors.

PORCH-SITTING was a pastime. After supper, folks ambled out to their front or side porches. Sometimes they walked over to their neighbors' porches.

FUNERAL PROCESSIONS Children growing up the first half of the 20th century watched their parents pull off the road when meeting a funeral procession.

FULL SERVICE GAS STATIONS - the stations of olden days washed the windshield, checked the oil, tires and water, and threw in a map, all for free.

School & Church

THE PLEDGE OF ALLEGIANCE in school

GOD IN SCHOOLS

CHALKBOARDS replaced with SMART boards - Once as synonymous with school as yellow buses and navy uniforms, walking into a classroom with a chalkboard in 2014 is a bit like entering a Neolithic cave. SMART Boards, created by the SMART Technologies company, are currently installed in 2.5 million K-12 classrooms around the world, with just over one million boards installed in the U.S. alone. They are basically large, wall-mounted touchscreen computers.

COVERING YOUR TEXTBOOKS for school with your moms brown paper bags

SPIRAL NOTEBOOKS replaced with iPads

FLOPPY DISKS replaced with external hard drives

RUBBER ELASTIC STRAPS to keep all your books together

DRESSING UP FOR CHURCH on Sunday.

BOWING OUR HEADS AT THE NAME OF JESUS - This is another act of reverence that helps to restore the honor our Lord deserves in a culture that often uses His name as a profanity. Fasting until Communion. Refraining from food and drink, not just an hour before receiving the Eucharist, but from the beginning of the day, was once the rule. Catholics who have returned to the old custom find it a meaningful way of exercising self-discipline and honoring the Lord in the Eucharist

MEATLESS FRIDAYS. When the bishops in America relaxed the traditional obligation to abstain from meat on Fridays (except those in Lent), they nevertheless insisted that we should continue to make some act of penance on that day. Though many Catholics no longer bother, many others have found that the small sacrifice of a meatless Friday bears important spiritual rewards for those who tend to feast every other day of the week.

SAYING GRACE AT MEALS - If God has graciously provided us food and everything else we have, the least we can do at every meal is to take time to say thanks.

WEARING A LACE COVER on our heads for church

BLUE LAWS --known also as Sunday laws-- are laws designed to restrict or ban some or all Sunday activities for religious standards, particularly the observance of a day of worship or rest. Blue laws may also restrict shopping or ban sale of certain items on specific days, most often on Sundays in the western world

MULTIPLE POPES - History has turned losing popes into Antipopes. But during the era in which they existed, there was no such thing as an Antipope. Between the years 200 and 1450, regional factions and political differences generated multiple popes dozens of times, each time vying for the head of the church. One of the most deplorable stories of papal succession is when Pope Benedict VI was imprisoned and murdered by the followers of Boniface VII. Boniface VII plundered the treasury at the Vatican Basilica and went into exile for a decade as Benedict VII quietly ruled over the church. Returning to Rome 10 years later, Boniface VII overpowered John XIV, literally, and forced him into the dungeons, where he later died. Being indirectly responsible for the deaths of two popes, Boniface's reign was short as he was killed in the year 985, "due in all probability to violence, the body of Boniface was exposed to the insults of the populace, dragged through the streets of the city, and finally, naked and covered in wounds, flung under the statue of Marcus

Aurelius." History labeled Boniface VII an
Antipope after his death.

HOLY WARS - In 1929, the Lateran Treaty
officially positioned the Vatican City as neutral in
international relations. On and off for a thousand
years prior, the head of the Catholic Church
didn't declare war on other nations, but declared
"Crusades" against other nations, forcing
conversions of the infidels at the end of a sword.
The First Crusade was ordered by Pope Urban II
in the year 1095, not to be confused with the
Crusade of 1101, directed by Urban II's
successor, Pope Paschal II... Not to be
confused with the Second Crusade, ordered in
the year 1145 by Pope Eugene III... Not to be
confused with the Third Crusade, engineered by
Pope Gregory VIII.

MARRIED PRIESTS - Peter, the first leader of
the Church, was a married man. The first written
regulation regarding married priests was the
Council of Elvira in the year 306. Not forbidding
marriage, mind you, but declaring that priests
and other elders of the church are to "abstain
completely from sexual intercourse with their
wives and from the procreation of children."
(Insert your no sex during marriage joke here.) A
hundred years later, the Council of Carthage
decreed no "conjugal relations" of any type were
allowed. Decrees, canons, announcements,

councils, all continued to try to curb the sexual appetite of the priests until the First Lateran Council of 1123, finally stating once and for all that "we forbid priests, deacons, subdeacons, and monks to have concubines or enter into the contract of marriage." A thousand years later, the clergy still struggles with the question of marriage, for every couple of years a high profile case of a clergyman with a secret family hits the media. One of the most recent examples was the 2012 resignation of Auxiliary Bishop of Los Angeles Gabino Zavala, resigning after the existence of a secret wife and 2 children was discovered.

DEAD (UNBAPTIZED) BABIES GO TO HELL - In 2007, Pope Benedict XVI decreed that unbaptized babies most probably go to heaven, "reflecting a growing awareness of God's mercy," which is almost certainly the polar opposite of the church's teachings for nearly the 1,500 years prior. For during the 5th Century, St. Augustine concluded that "infants who die without baptism are consigned to hell." Relenting a bit during the 13th Century, church leaders decreed that unbaptized infants were in limbo, deprived of the vision of God, yet did not suffer because they were unaware of what they were deprived of. Which begs the question: Is 2007 the year that God swooped down from heaven and rose up all the dead unbaptized babies from hell? Or limbo?

NON-INFALLIBILITY - With all of the strife and instability of the Middle Ages, even the Popes were scrutinized for their leadership. In a clever idea spawned from Pope Gregory VII in the year 1075, the Dictatus Papae declared that nobody could judge a Pope except for God (amongst other things, including Princes should kiss the Pope's feet). By introducing the concept of Papal Infallibility, which was cemented dogmatically by the First Vatican Council, a Pope is preserved from the possibility of error.

Without becoming too blasphemous, doesn't infallibility open up a whole new can of worms, like does the Pope become infallible at the coronation? At birth? When he becomes a priest? And secondly, when a Pope apologizes for mistakes of earlier Papal administrations, how can you apologize for mistakes that technically didn't exist because the previous administration was infallible? And currently, are you still infallible in retirement? And, and, oh forget it, my head hurts.

INDULGENCES - Today an indulgence is an extra-sacramental remission of the temporal punishment due, in God's justice, to sin that has been forgiven, which remission is granted by the Church. That's nice. But during the more, well, corrupt, days of the church, indulgences were monetary purchases of salvation. The practice of using indulgences can be traced back to the 6th Century, but they had been so abused that the topic was one of the pillars of reform written about in Martin Luther's 95 Theses in 1517. No matter how you feel about the church currently, no church leaders are brazen enough in the age of the internet to promise the congregation eternal life in exchange for cash.

MASS IN LATIN - When you worship the Lord today, no matter what your Christian denomination, it is assumed that you do so in your own language. Makes sense, but that hasn't always been the case. Between 1570 and 1962, nearly 400 years, most Catholics around the world celebrated Mass in Latin. Today Latin is still the official language in Vatican City, and the business of the church is done in Latin, but the Vatican II Council allowed masses to be more accessible to the scripture by making the language vernacular. Despite the common sense of worshiping in your native tongue, the Latin Mass is making a bit of a comeback in conservative Catholic parishes.

PRIEST SUICIDE - Heaven is a great place. As a matter of fact, it was such a great place compared to the squalor and despair of the old world, priests often committed suicide to be with the Lord in the afterlife. It wasn't until the 4th

Century A.D. that St. Augustine condemned the practice, not so much due to theology, but due to the fact that Christians were offing themselves in such large numbers. For a thousand years after, suicide was discouraged because if there were no priests, there would be no one to lead the congregation. By the 13th Century, St. Thomas Aquinas had fortified the church's stance against suicide based on the theological argument that taking one's own life was a sin against God. Civil and criminal laws followed outlining suicide as a crime in multiple Christian nations

UNCIRCUMCISION - Why don't you males out there have your foreskin? Well, due to religious beliefs, that is the conventional wisdom. In reality the Catholic Church doesn't really care either way. Way back in the year 50 A.D., the Council of Jerusalem rejected circumcision as a requirement for Gentile converts to Christianity. Actually, the topic of circumcision was one of the first subjects that differentiated Jews and early Christians in the 1st Century A.D. In the New Testament there are contradictory statements regarding circumcision, and some Catholic scholars consider male circumcision an act of mutilation. If that's the case, then why does no one today reject circumcision? Well, many Catholics still refer back to the tenants of Mosaic Law back in the Old Testament, despite that being the wrong interpretation of the situation because New Testament tenants are supposed to supersede the tenants of the Old Testament. If Paul wrote to the Corinthians "circumcision is nothing and uncircumcision is nothing, but keeping the commandments of God is what matters" 1 Cor 7:19, why is there so much confusion over circumcision's importance? Today circumcision is mostly performed for health reasons.

SIGN OF THE CROSS – remember when we passed a church, it was common practice to make the sign of the cross.

John Louis Sublett

Entertainment

DRIVE-IN MOVIES - Distant memories still exist in my mind of a time when we loaded up the car for a night at the drive-in movies. I recall the time my buddies and I sneaked in the drive-in hidden inside of the trunk of an old beat up car.

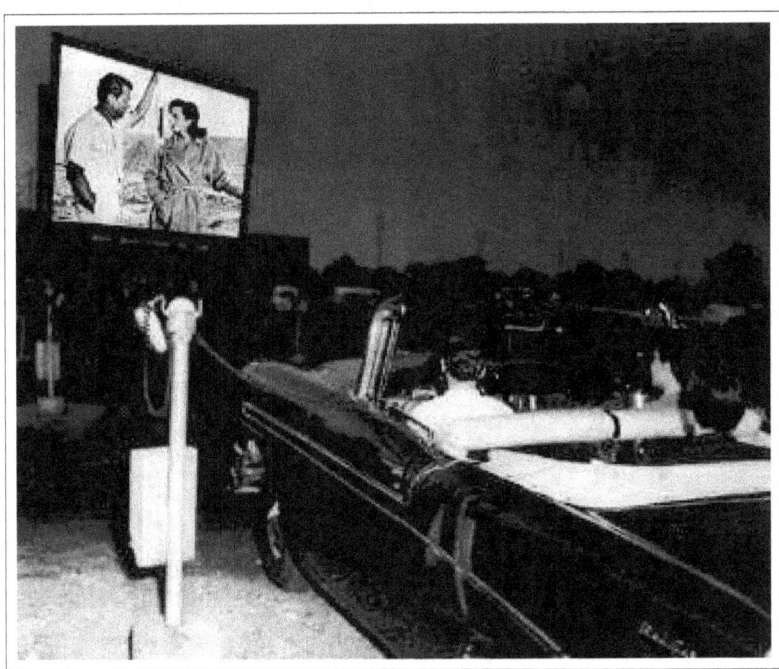

The idea of the drive-in theater didn't really take off until after World War II. The baby boomer generation made it a hit. In the 1950s more people attended the drive-in than the indoor theater. The drive-ins had playgrounds for the kids where they could play before the movie and during the intermission. You didn't need a baby-sitter and the cost of the family outing was relatively cheap.

The drive-in was a perfect date location with the parking for a little necking already provided. Steamy windshields were evident in all directions.

Families could spend a low-budget entertainment evening at the drive-in theater. People brought lawn chairs to watch the movies under the stars while the very little ones slept in the car with their favorite blanket and pillow. Many families would bring snacks from home to save even more money. It was not unusual to have special nights where you could bring a carload for five dollars or even less.

HOLDING LIGHTERS AT CONCERTS: This was done to show appreciation for a song. Or something. I did it because the guy next to me was doing it. But holy fire hazard! Today, some people raise their opened cell phones in this manner. Or display the lighter application on their iPhones. But is this because of the safety element, or because now more people carry phones than lighters?

WATCHING COMMERCIALS: Commercials were short advertisements that allowed you to get up for a snack during shows. There was no fast forward option. No pause!

BUYING PORN MAGAZINES: These were glossy periodicals that contained photos of nudes engaged in activities of prurient interest. (But I bought them for the articles!) They lived behind black Plexiglass at the corner store. And you needed ID. Now, with the internet, who needs magazines?

LISTENING TO TAPES AND CD'S: I know this one might be complicated to understand, but way back when, you actually had to purchase music on CD's and audio cassette tapes; we devoted shelves and binders to storing these objects. They usually came in plastic cases that cracked in two and then littered the floor of your car.

RENTING MOVIES & LATE FEES: Video rental places were storefronts that stocked DVD's and VHS tapes. Empty boxes lined the walls so that you could read the literature on the back. The boxes supposedly represented what the rental shop had in stock, but it wasn't a fail-proof system.

READING NEWSPAPERS: These were disposable stacks of paper that did not require any source of electricity. They contained news and interesting stories, but they could not be updated instantly (like we do with the internet today): If you wanted to find out what happened today, you'd have to wait for tomorrow's paper.

WATCHING PROGRAMMED TV: Back in the dark times, you had to watch shows when the network wanted you to watch them. That was it. That was the ONLY option. You either went out or you watched Saturday Night Live. Or you figured out how to program your VCR ... You see, VCR's were these devices which ... uh, forget it.

CB RADIOS – Citizen Band Radios. If you were one of the cool ones you had a CB mounted under the dash of your car, but if you had the latest, you had one that mounted in the trunk of your car and all the controls were on the microphone. In the 1970's, CB's were like the facebook and twitter of today, they were the social media. We used them more for fun than anything else – remember the lingo . . .

- Bear Taking Pictures - Police officer with a radar

- Smokey Bear - Law enforcement officer

- Smokey in the Bush - Law enforcement officer hiding

- Plain Brown Wrapper - Unmarked police car

- Got Your Ears On? - Are you listening?

- Handle - Nickname

- Breaker - Someone wanting to join a conversation on a certain channel

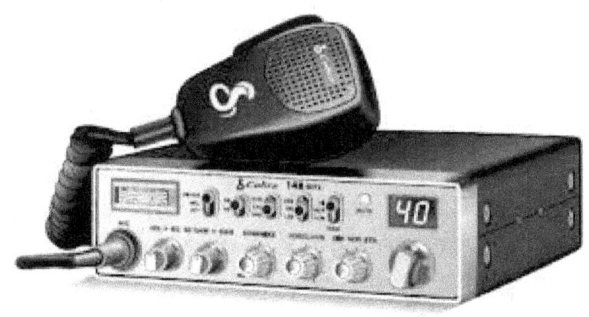

PUNCHBOARDS - were the descendants of handmade lottery game boards, which were used in the U.S. as early as the eighteenth century. Lotteries were popular at the time, but they required a large number of ticket-buyers to be successful. Somewhere along the line an enterprising tavern-keeper found a way that he could run a lottery for just a few customers, or even just one. He constructed a game board out of wood, probably about a half an inch thick and 8 inches square. He drilled a number of holes in the board, filling each with a slip of rolled or folded paper. He probably also lettered a sign proclaiming the prizes available. He then charged patrons a fixed sum of money (probably a penny or a nickel) for a chance at several prizes or sums of cash. The patron would use a nail to push one of the slips of paper out of its hole. Each slip of paper had a number printed on it, and if the customer's number corresponded to a number listed as a winner, the customer won that prize. The punchboard was born.

Early in the nineteenth century, the lottery game board became very scarce, due largely to the greed of the operators. Gamblers realized that all too often the "big" prizes ended up in the operator's pockets. Since the boards were hand-made, usually by the operator, he could very easily know where the winning tickets were and punch them out when no one was looking. If anyone asked who won the big prize, he would just claim that it was a stranger and put a new board up the next day. Some operators found this procedure to be too time consuming, and just didn't bother to put any winning tickets on the board at all. In both cases, the players got wise and quit playing.

In the late 1800s, punchboards resurfaced with a new, modern appearance. The new punchboards were constructed out of cardboard, with paper covering the fronts and backs of the holes. This added level of complexity was intended to prevent the operator from discovering where the winners were and tampering with the board. The boards were sold with a metal stylus or "punch" for the players to use. Players responded, and the games began to appear again in the bars, drugstores, and barber shops of America. The Punchboard or Salesboard was patented in 1905 by C. A. Brewer and C. G. Scannell of Chicago. Even though the equivalent of punchboards had been around for many years, they had never been available in such a neat and portable form. The invention of board stuffing machines and ticket folding and plaiting machines in the late 1910s was probably the key factor which allowed the punchboard industry to flourish.

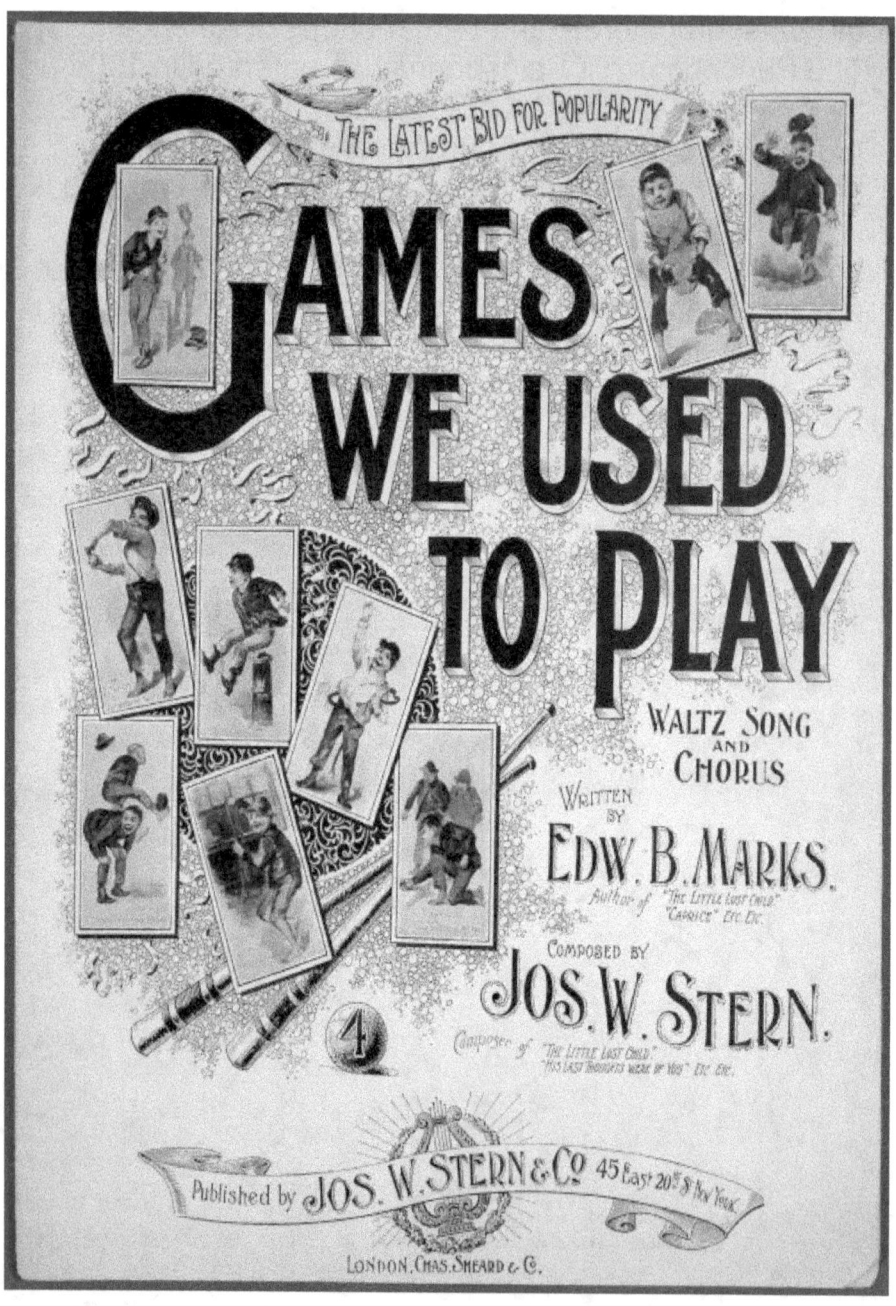

Street Games

1. **Punchball** - is a sport spawned by and similar to baseball, but without a pitcher, catcher, or bat. The "batter" essentially plays "fungo" without a bat, bouncing or tossing up the ball and then using a volleyball-type approach to put the ball (usually a spaldeen or pensie pinkie) in play, punching the ball with his closed fist. Stealing and bunting are not allowed.

2. **Johnny on the Pony** (Buck Buck) - One version of the game is played when "one player climbs another's back" and the climber guesses "the number of certain objects out of sight. Another version of the game is played with one group of players climbing on the backs of a second group in order to build as large a pile as possible or to cause the supporting players to collapse.

3. **Hot Beans and Butter** (Hot Buttered Beans) The rules were that a child hid a belt somewhere and everyone searched for it, with hints of, "You are getting warmer" or "You are getting colder." Then when someone found the belt they could

whip the crap out of everyone else until they made it to a designated "home base." We played all the time, all you needed was one belt. Talk about speed and agility training – get away or get whipped!

4. **Red Light – Green Light – One – Two – Three** - One person is designated as "it" and plays the part of the stop light. The other kids line up about 20 feet away from "it." Facing away from the other kids, "it' calls out "Green light!" The other kids move toward "it." "It" then calls out "Red light!" and turns around quickly. Any of the kids who are caught moving must go back to the start line. Play continues until someone reaches and tags "it." That person then becomes "it." The trick to winning this game is to move smoothly so that you can freeze instantly until you are within reach of "it."

5. **Mother, May I** - This game is set up in the same way as Red Light Green Light. One person in the group asks the person in the front, "Mother, may I take <insert number> steps forward?" The person at the front then says, "Yes, you may." or "No, you may not." You can vary your requests by including options such as taking baby steps, spinning steps, leaps or whatever strikes your fancy. Again, the first person to tag the person in the front wins and is the next person in the front.

6. **Stickball** – (equipment needed - Spalding ball, a
    sawed off broom or mop handle with a taped up
    handle) a street game related to baseball,
    usually formed as a pick-up game played in large
    cities in the Northeastern United States,
    especially New York City and Philadelphia. The
    equipment consists of a broom handle and a
    rubber ball, typically a spaldeen, pensy pinky,
    high bouncer or tennis ball. The rules come from
    baseball and are modified to fit the situation, for
    example, a manhole cover may be used as a
    base, or buildings for foul lines. The game is a
    variation of stick and ball games dating back to
    at least the 1750s. This game was widely
    popular among youths growing up from the 19th
    century until the 1980s.

7. **Stoopball** - is a game that is played by throwing a ball against a stoop (stairs leading up to a building) on the pavement in front of a building. The game is also known as "Off the Point". Historically, it has been popular in Brooklyn and other inner cities. It first became popular after World War II.

8. **Skully** (also called skelly, skellies, skelsy, skellzies, scully, loadies, tops or caps) is a children's game played on the streets of New York City and other urban areas. Sketched on the street usually in chalk, a skully or skelly board allows a game for two to six players. A sidewalk is sometimes used, offering greater protection from vehicular traffic; however, the asphalt on a typical city street is smoother and provides better game play than a bumpy cement sidewalk. Game time varies, but a match of two to three players is usually completed in 20 minutes. Local variations in rules are common and make it difficult to document the game. Rule variations are agreed upon by players before

starting a game, especially when players from different neighborhoods play against each other..

9. **Boxball** - boxball transforms two sidewalk squares into an outdoor version of ping-pong or, perhaps more accurately, a postage-stamp-sized game of tennis. Each player serves, volleys, and defends his square. The lines (or "cracks") around the concrete define the court; the seam between the two squares is the imaginary net. Players choose or volley for first serve. Depending on the neighborhood, serve is maintained by the winner of the volley or rotated every five points. In some games, only the server wins a point; others play so that either player can win any point. Twenty-one is usually the winning score, with the requirement of winning by two points. The ball is slapped back and forth between boxes with an open palm. Slap the ball into your opponent's box; he or she returns it back to your box after one bounce or on the fly. If you step into the playing court, fail to return a shot, or if your return shot's first bounce lands out of your opponents box, you lose the volley.

10. **Red Rover** (come on over) or Break the Chain -
    2 teams,the team that was "UP" called an
    opposing player over,if they broke through their
    team was "UP",if they didn't than they were
    captured and joined the opposing team who then
    called another player over,until everyone was on
    one team and you started over by dividing up
    again.(red rover, red rover let Johnny come
    over)

11. **Ringolevio** - is a children's game which may be
    played anywhere but which originates in the

teeming streets of New York City, and is known to have been played there at least as far back as before World War I. It is one of the many variations of tag. It requires close team work and near-military strategy. In some quarters, this game is known as Manhunt, which is really another game with different rules.

12. **Kick the Can** - (also known as Pom Pom and Tip the can) is a children's game related to tag, hide and seek, and capture the flag which can be played outdoors, with as many as three to a few dozen players. The game is one of skill, strategy, and stealth as well as fitness.

13. **Hopscotch** - is a children's game that can be played with several players or alone. Hopscotch is a popular playground game in which players toss a small object into numbered spaces of a pattern of rectangles outlined on the ground and then hop or jump through the spaces to retrieve the object.

14. **Double Dutch** - is a game in which two long jump ropes turning in opposite directions are jumped by one or more players jumping simultaneously. Played with two skipping ropes. Two people holding the ends. The ropes were turned simultaneously, right then left. A third person would jump in either from next to one of the turners, or if you were really good you could jump in right in the middle of the rope and jump over the ropes without tripping. You could also do kind of a step hop skip, and if there were others waiting a turn, you could run out of the ropes, again without tripping or stopping the ropes.

We did rhymes, but the idea was to skip as long

as possible, if you stumbled you had to take an end. In America, double Dutch began in the cities. It is popular worldwide. Competitions in double Dutch range from block parties to the world level. During the spring of 2009, double Dutch became a varsity sport in New York City public high schools.

15. **Steal the Bacon** - is a tag-based children's game, in which teams try to steal a flag or other item (the "bacon") from the field without being tagged.

16. **Ace-King-Queen** - Chinese handball (known in its 3-or-more-player forms as Ace-King-Queen, King(s), Down the River or Slugs), is a form of American handball popular on the streets of New York City, Philadelphia, and Bridgewater, NJ during the 1960s,'70s, and '80s and is still played today, mostly in New York City, Philadelphia, and San Diego. Different variations are played around the world. Its defining feature is that, unlike traditional handball, in Chinese or indirect handball, for a shot to be valid, the ball must hit the ground before it hits the wall. It would seem that this game, or mini variants of it, were highly popular almost worldwide in the 1950s, 1960s and 1970s.

17. **Off the Wall** - There are actually two versions of Off the Wall. The normal game is closely related

to stoopball, with anywhere from one to perhaps six players per team. Basic baseball rules apply and you either run out the hit or get bases depending on the number of bounces. It is a classic of street play that can adapted to a variety of locales. The other game known as of Off the Wall is often played in school yards while finishing lunch. It might be described as the lunatic version, definitely more colorful and clearly not a team sport. Rules are almost non-existent, with every man for himself. Here's an attempt at some guidelines: the guy who has the ball runs up and throws it against a wall. All players in the field then rush over and attempt to catch the ball on the fly. They scramble, bump, and knock into each other, trying to perform the deed. If it drops, the thrower gets another turn. If someone successfully catches the ball, he immediately dashes up and throws it against the wall. That's about it. If you want to get organized, you can play for points, get one each time you throw an uncaught ball. However, the real intention isn't to rack up points, rather it's to knock the heck out of each other while hanging out at school and playing ball.

18. **Marbles** – all marbles games always involve
moving marbles around. You roll, toss, or flick a
shooter marble called a shooter, taw, or boss.
The shooter marble is usually larger than other
marbles, and the target marbles are called mibs
or kimmies. Some games involve a taw line,
which players stand behind when shooting.
Players take turns shooting marbles until ll of the
target marbles are gone, or until players decide
to quit. Sometimes players take more than one
turn in a row when they are successful at hitting
the opponents marbles.

19. **Hit the Stick (Coin)** - Neither speed, strength, nor agility matter here; careful aim and a light touch are the important skills. Hit the Coin and Hit the Stick require two players, a relatively level, uncracked two-square stretch of sidewalk, and a coin (usually a penny) or a Good Humor ice cream stick. The players stand at either end of two concrete squares with a coin or stick placed directly in the center seam. The object is to hit the coin or stick with the ball and, even better, attempt to flip it over. Each hit brings one point, each flip is worth two, with play ending once a player reaches 11 or 21. Some find Hit the Stick more appealing because it's more of a kick to see the stick flip up and turn in the air than checking to see if the penny or nickel is heads of tails. Historically, some would play with the winner buying ice cream, while others just for the fun of hitting the stick

20. **Freeze Tag** - Also known as Stuck in the Mud, Scarecrow, Sticky-Glue, Zombie Tag, players who are tagged are "stuck in the mud" or "frozen" and must stand in place with their arms stretched out until they are unfrozen. An unstuck player can perform an action to unfreeze them, such as tagging them, crawling between their legs,or "flushing" them by hitting their outstretched hand ("Toilet tag").

21. **Simon Says -** This game can be played anywhere, even in a car or other small space. One person is Simon and starts by saying, "Simon says, '<insert action here>.'" Everyone must then do the action. However, if Simon makes an action request without saying, "Simon says" to begin the request, anyone who does that action is out. The last person still playing in the end will be Simon for the next round.

22. **Clap and Rhyme** - (mainly a girls game) - Waiting on line at camp, sitting on the stoop, waiting to go into school, anytime we had time, we could break into a clapping rhyme. Boys had to carry a ball, but for us no equipment was required. All you needed was a friend who either knew the rhymes and moves or was willing to learn them.

Each rhyme had its own variations, where you'd pat your shoulders, hands or thighs and clap hands with your partner. One or two hands at a time, backs of hands, palms, double claps, hands up, hands down, all the little variations that made each song distinct. You'd play and play, trying to get faster both in the song and claps . Here is one of the famous rhymes . . .

Miss Mary Mack, Mack, Mack,
All dressed in black, black, black,
With silver buttons, buttons, buttons
All down her back, back, back
She asked her mother, mother, mother,

Lost Traditions

For fifty cents, cents, cents,
To see the elephants, elephants, elephants,
Jump over the fence, fence, fence,
They went so high, high, high
They reached the sky, sky, sky
They never came back, back, back,
Till The Fourth of July, ly, ly.

23. **Jacks** - The game is played outdoors on a
    smooth surface such as asphalt or concrete, or
    indoors on an uncarpeted floor. There are
    usually anywhere from two to six individual
    players. Equipment includes 15 jacks and one
    small ball. Two players sit face to face; more
    than two sit in a circle. Deciding who goes first is
    optional, everything from eenie-meenie-meinie-
    moe to throwing the jacks up in the air and trying
    to catch as many as possible with both hands
    together, thumb to thumb, palms down. Whoever
    catches the most jacks goes first. The player up
    gathers all of the jacks in one hand, gives them a
    gentle toss and scatters them onto the ground,
    anywhere inside the space encircled by her and
    her opponents. Following that, she tosses the

ball into the air. The object of the game is to pick up the designated number of jacks with one hand and catch the ball on the first bounce in that same hand. It starts with one jack at a time (onesies), then two jacks (twosies), right on up till the player misses. She continues at that number on her next turn. Then the next player goes. The game continues until someone succeeds at picking up the ball and all of the jacks at once on a single bounce. Frankly,

24. **7UP Game** - This game was played in school when the teacher had a few minutes til class was out. All kids put their heads down on their desk and the teacher picks 7 kids to come around and tap one person each on the head. Then the "tappers" go to the front and all the kids put their heads up. The ones that were tapped stand up, and one by one they have one guess to see if they can pick the person who tapped them. If they get it right, they take that player's spot in front and become a "tapper" in the next round. If they don't guess correctly, the person at the front stays in the line and gets to "tap" again.

John Louis Sublett

Military Life

1. Breaking Starch - referring to the tradition of starching utility uniforms to the point that it was necessary to shove a broomstick down each leg of the trousers to separate the fabric before they could be donned.

2. Open-bay barracks

3. Spit-shined boots

4. Regular inspections in Class A uniforms, too, and weekly battalion-sized retreat parades, complete with a band and passing in review.

5. Total Victory - America used to fight and win wars to total victory, even when we didn't quite get the enemies right!

6. Soldiers don't march much anymore - One of the classic images of an Army post is of bodies of Soldiers marching in formation. While the Army still teaches dismounted drill, its use is rapidly fading.

7. The daily 'Police Call' – cleaning up around thr baracks, picking up the cigarette butts.

John Louis Sublett

Death & Funerals

1. **Keening (Death Wail)** - The death wail is a keening, mourning lament, generally performed in ritual fashion soon after the death of a member of a family or tribe. Examples of death wails have been found in numerous societies, including among the Celts and various indigenous peoples of Asia and Africa.
The Irish tradition of keening over the body at the burial is distinct from the wake - the practice of watching over the corpse - which took place the night before the burial. The "keen" itself is thought to have been constituted of stock poetic elements (the listing of the genealogy of the deceased, praise for the deceased, emphasis on the woeful condition of those left behind etc.) set to vocal lament. While generally carried out by one or several women, a chorus may have been intoned by all present. Physical movements involving rocking, kneeling or clapping accompanied the keening woman ("bean caoinadh") who was often paid for her services. After consistent opposition from the Roman Catholic Church in Ireland (Synods opposed the practice in 1631, 1748 and 1800) that went so far as to recommend excommunication for offenders, the practice became extinct; the Church's position is however unlikely to have

been the sole cause. Although some recordings have been made and the practice has been documented up to recent times, it is generally considered to be extinct.

Keening at a Wake

2. **Postmortem Portraits (memento mori)** - Prior to 1839 portraits were painted, but with the invention of the daguerreotype photograph, portraiture become more affordable and accessible. This meant that the middle class

could now afford to have pictures taken to memorialize their loved ones — their dead loved ones, that is, and particularly infants and children. Sometimes pupils were painted over the closed eyelids so that the eyes looked open. With the invention of the carte de visite in the middle of the century came multiple prints so that families could share pictures of their dead children with other family members and friends. Since most children would not have had their images captured prior to their untimely deaths, it makes perfect sense; although the practice would seem utterly taboo in contemporary Western culture.

The living dead - Since the idea of postmortem portraits was to have something to remember the deceased by, there was often staging and post-photo work done to achieve the effect of life. Bodies were posed in lifelike positions, surrounded by family, children holding favorite toys, and eyes often propped open. Sometimes, pupils were painted on in the studio and rosy cheeks were added to the image of the corpse.

3. **Coal for Jewelry** - The material most prized to show grief was lignite, also known as jet, a fossilized form of coal. Jet is deep, dark and somber. In the first phase of mourning, jet jewelry was the only ornamentation women were allowed to wear.

4. **Funeral Biscuits** - Small cakes, known as "funeral biscuits" were wrapped in white paper and sealed with black sealing wax and given to guests as favors. Commemorative eating and drinking customs at funerals go back so far in time that Paleolithic humans are believed to have dined on the corpse itself before they buried it. Those ancestors -- we now know them as "cave men" -- were the first humans to perceive some higher meaning in death and to ceremonially entomb their dead. It's likely that eating a bit of a deceased loved one was an effort to both honor and incorporate their essence into one's own. Anthropologists believe

this grisly habit evolved into the somewhat more civilized mourning practices throughout medieval Europe and ultimately gave rise to the "funeral biscuits" so popular in the Victorian age. Emerging from the Middle Ages in old Germany, for instance, was the funeral tradition of eating "corpse cakes" that symbolically mirrored the act of eating the deceased. After the body had been washed and laid in its coffin, the woman of the house prepared leavened dough and placed it to rise on the linen-covered chest of the corpse. It was believed the dough "absorbed" some of the deceased's personal qualities that were, in turn, passed on to mourners who ate the corpse cakes.

Funeral Biscuits

5. Widow's Walk

A widow's walk also known as a "widow's watch" (or roofwalk) is a railed rooftop platform often with a small enclosed cupola frequently found on 19th-century North American coastal houses. A popular romantic myth holds that the platform was used to observe vessels at sea. The name is said to come from the wives of mariners, who would watch for their spouses' return, often in vain as the ocean took the lives of the mariners, leaving the women widows. In other coastal communities, the platforms were called Captain's Walk, as they topped the homes of the more successful captains; supposedly, ship owners and captains would use them to search the horizon for ships due in port.

The scene in Mary Poppins where Admiral Boom warns Burt about foul weather ahead is an elaborate 'Widow Walk'

6. **Buried Facing East** - In many cemeteries, the vast majority of graves are oriented in such a manner that the bodies lie with their heads to the West and their feet to the East. This very old custom appears to originate with the Pagan sun worshippers, but is primarily attributed to Christians who believe that the final summons to Judgment will come from the East.

7. **Sign of the Cross** - We always stopped walking on the sidewalk if a funeral passed by....and we would make the sign of the cross as it passed

8. **Black Ribbons on the Door** - Putting a flower on the door of the person who died for people to know. A wreath of laurel, yew or boxwood tied with crape or black ribbons was hung on the front door to alert passersby that a death had occurred.

9. **Security of the Wake** - The wake also served as a safeguard from burying someone who was not dead, but in a coma.

10. **Bricking-Over** - Grave robbery by the "Resurrectionist Men", often doctors themselves was a problem in the 19th century as medical schools needed fresh cadavers for dissection classes. "Bricking-over" a grave was a way of guaranteeing some security after death.

11. **Family Photographs** - were also sometimes turned face-down to prevent any of the close relatives and friends of the deceased from being possessed by the spirit of the dead

.

12. **Funerals at Home** - For the most part it used to be the case that in the 19th century people would die at home; funerals would happen at home. A middle-class house would typically have two parlors: a front parlor and a back parlor. The front parlor was a special formal room where you'd have major family rituals like marriages and funerals. People had a much more direct and visceral contact with death.

13. **Waking** - The body was watched over every minute until burial, hence the custom of "waking".

14. **Scents** - The use of flowers and candles helped to mask unpleasant odors in the room before embalming became common.

15. **Long Wakes** - Most wakes also lasted 3-4 days to allow relatives to arrive from far away.

16. **Sati** - was a Hindu funeral custom, now a serious criminal act in India, in which a widow would throw herself on her dead husband's funeral pyre to commit suicide. The act of sati

was supposed to take place voluntarily, and from existing accounts, most of them were indeed voluntary. The act may have been expected of widows in some communities. The extent to which any social pressures or expectations should be considered as compulsion has been the matter of much debate in modern times. It is frequently stated that a widow could expect little of life after her husband's death, especially if she was childless. However, there were also instances where the wish of the widow to commit sati was not welcomed by others, and where efforts were made to prevent the death.

17. **Wearing the Hair of the Dead** - during the second stage of mourning one could wear a piece of jewelry if it contained, or was made of, hair. That would be human hair. That would be human hair taken from the deceased love one. Brooches, bracelets, rings, chains and buckles were all made of hair; sometimes there was just a bit enclosed in a hollow band or brooch, other times, the hair was crafted into a piece of its own.

18. **Hanging Coffins** - are an ancient funeral custom of some minority groups, especially the Bo people of southern China. Coffins of various shapes were mostly carved from one whole piece of wood. Hanging coffins either lie on beams projecting outward from vertical faces

such as mountains, are placed in caves in the face of cliffs, or sit on natural rock projections on mountain faces.
It was said that the hanging coffins could prevent bodies from being taken by beasts and also bless the soul eternally.

19. **Widow's Weeds** - Cloaked in heavy veils and bonnets - A widow was to wear a bonnet of heavy crepe and a veil to cover the face for the first three months. At the end of three months the veil was to be worn from the back of the bonnet for another nine months. Altogether, restrictive mourning dress, known as widow's weeds, was to be worn for a minimum of two years, although many widows chose to shun color forever.

20. **Stop the Clock** - When someone died in the house and there was a clock in the room, you had to stop the clock at the death hour or the family of the household would have bad luck.

21. **Cemetery Picnics** - Middle-class families often took outings to these graveyards on weekends.

22. **Cover the Mirrors** - Mirrors were covered because it was thought that the next person to see themselves in the mirror would be the next to die. Reflections in the mirror were believed to be a projection of your soul (that's why Dracula never saw his reflection) and the ghost of the recently deceased would linger about the house and if he saw a reflection he would grab that person's soul and take it to the afterlife with him. It was believed that someone seeing their reflection in a room where someone has recently died, will soon die themselves.

23. **Feet First** - In both Europe and America in the 19th century, the deceased were always carried out of the house feet first so they wouldn't look back into the house and beckon to someone else, who would have to go along with them.

24. **Blindfold Death** - in the Northwestern Philippines they would blindfold their dead and place them next to the main entrance of the house. while their

25. **Last Smoke** – The Tinguian, a mountain tribe in the Philippines dress the dead body in their best clothes, sit them on a chair and place a lit cigarette in their lips.

26. **Tree Grave** - The Caviteño, who live near Manila, Philippines bury their dead in a hollowed-out tree trunk. When someone becomes ill, they select the tree where they will eventually be entombed.

27. **Segregated Cemeteries** – I am not talking about by race, we all know that has happened in our history, but many cemeteries back in the day had a segregated policy for men and women.

28. **Kitchen Death** - the Apayo, who live in the north, Philippines, bury their dead under the kitchen.

29. **Tree Trunk Burial** - The Caviteño, who live near Manila, bury their dead in a hollowed-out tree trunk. When someone becomes ill, they select the tree where they will eventually be entombed.

30. **Coffin Corner** - Many houses of the mid-to-late Victorian period have a special niche called a "coffin corner" cut into the stairwell so that the coffin could make the turn in the flight of stairs by fitting the head of the coffin into this little niche shelf.

31. **Showcase Window** - Some old homes also have a showcase window in the front of the house, a sort of bay window where the deceased could lie in state for people to pass by on the street and pay their respects.

32. **Maidens' Garlands** - These were formerly constructed to mark the death of a local person, usually but not exclusively female, who had led an unblemished life and had died unmarried. The garland was carried over the coffin at the funeral and then hung in the church, where it stayed until it rotted away. Methods of construction and exact details of the custom varied from place to place, but the following description is a reasonable synopsis:They are made of variegated colored paper, representing flowers, fastened to small sticks crossing each other at the top, and fixed at the bottom by a circular hoop. From the center is suspended the form of a woman's glove cut in white paper, on which the name and age of the deceased are sometimes written. They are made of variegated colored paper, representing flowers, fastened to small sticks crossing each other at the top, and fixed at the bottom by a circular hoop. From the center is suspended the form of a woman's glove cut in white paper, on which the name and age of the deceased are sometimes written.

33. **Green Funerals**. In the United States, more and

more people are opting for environmentally friendly burials. This means skipping embalming processes, nixing traditional concrete vaults and getting biodegradable, woven-willow caskets, which decompose into the ground. The Green Burial Council has approved 40 environmentally friendly cemeteries in the U.S. — way up from a decade ago. Another option: becoming a memorial "reef ball." A company called Eternal Reefs compresses remains into a sphere that is attached to a reef in the ocean, providing a habitat for sea life.

34. **Keep the Body Cool** - keeping the dead body of your loved one under the family home until enough money can be saved for a proper funeral celebration in Indonesia.

35. **Stop the Clock** - People stopped the clocks in the house at the time of death so they wouldn't have further bad luck.

36. **Two Year Mourning** - A widow was expected to stay in mourning for more than two years. For the first year and one day, she wore only dull black clothing without jewelry and a black cape that was her "weeping veil." The clothing became slightly more adorned and a little less crepe-covered as time went on; in a later stage of mourning, a woman could wear purple or gray.

37. **Clothing Style** - What style, material, and color a widow wore & for how long depended on who she was mourning a spouse, parent, child, sibling, grandparent, aunt/uncle, etc., and how long it had been since they died.

38. **Work** - Men could continue working after a loved one died, but women were expected to be isolated at home.

39. **Coffin Alarms** – this is where the term "Saved by the bell" came from - The fear of being buried alive was so severe that a device known as a coffin alarm was invented. The contraption was simply a bell attached to the headstone with a chain that connected to a ring placed on the finger of the corpse. (Gives the term "dead ringer" a whole new meaning.)

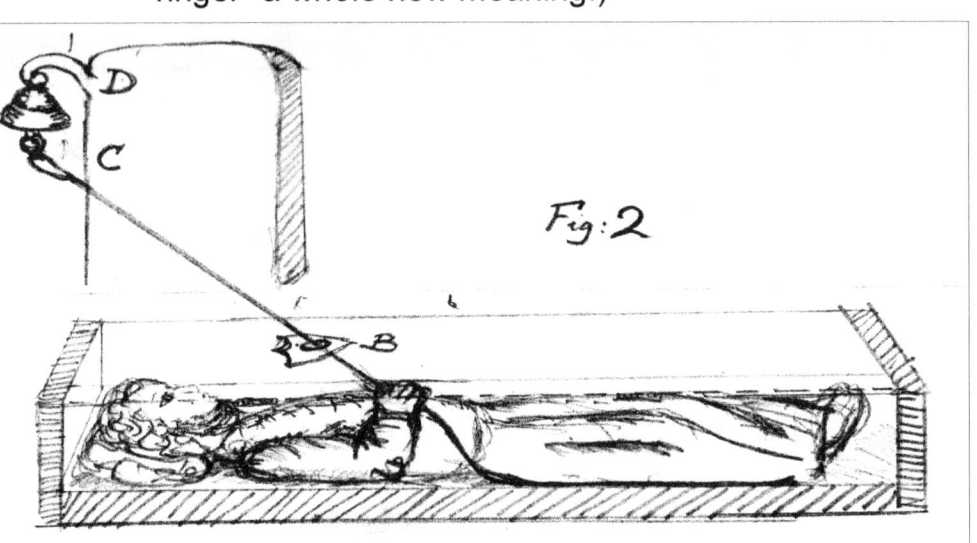

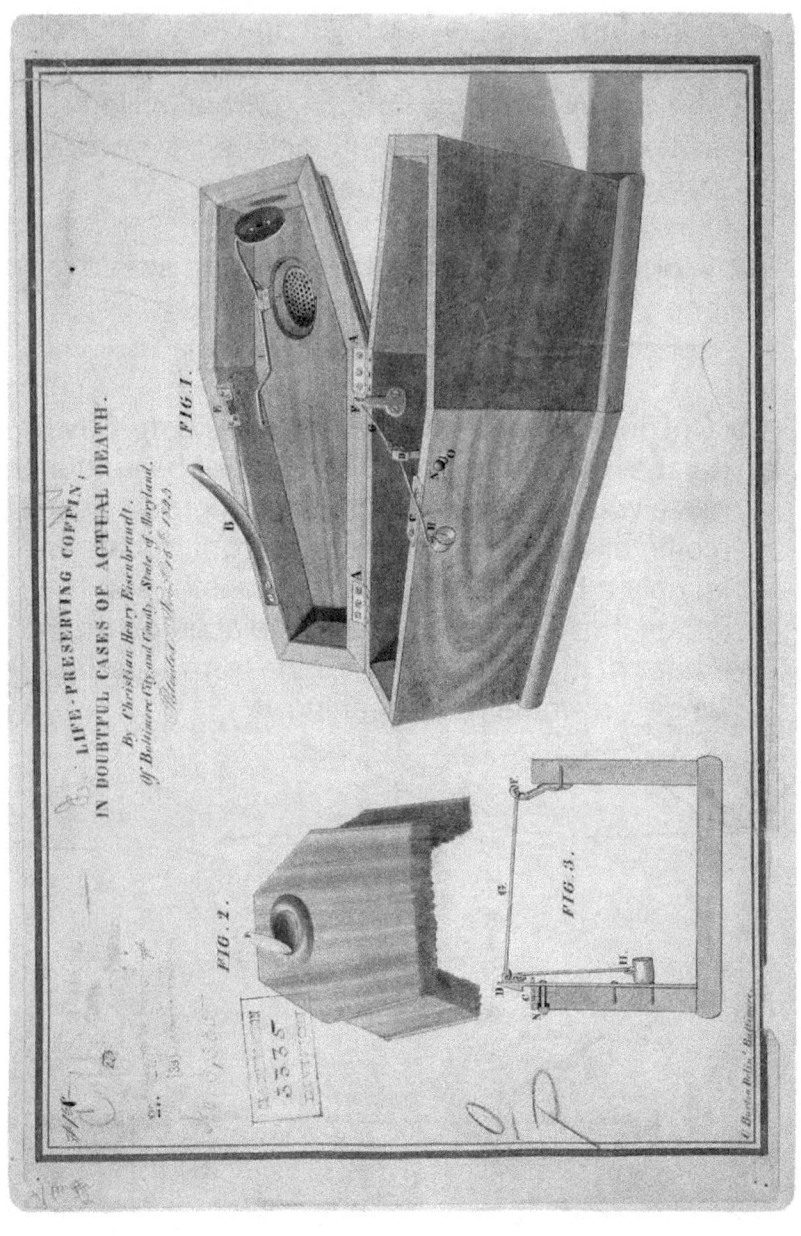

From the inventor . . .

To all whom it may concern Be it known that I, CHRISTIAN HENRY EISENBRANDT, of the city of Baltimore and State of Maryland, have invented a new and useful improvement in coffins, which I term a "life-preserving coffin in doubtful cases of death", and whereas there have been instances of human beings buried alive the inventor of this coffin has contrived an arrangement whereby any one who may not really have departed this life may by the slightest motion of either the head or hand acting upon a system of opening of the Collin-lid.

40. **Life Preserving Coffin** - The lid had a perforated air plate of metal, or any other suitable material, placed exactly over the mouth of the person, so as to allow breathing, if required. Over the last named plate, and outside of the lid, is placed another plate with a hinge, so it can be raised from the air plate, which may have the name and age engraved upon it.

41. **Death Masks** - A death mask is a wax or plaster cast made of a person's face following death. Death masks may be mementos of the dead, or be used for creation of portraits. It is sometimes possible to identify portraits that have been painted from death masks, because of the characteristic slight distortions of the features caused by the weight of the plaster during the making of the mold. In the tenth century in some European countries, it was common for death masks to be used as part of the effigy of the deceased, displayed at state funerals. During the eighteenth and nineteenth centuries they were also used to permanently record the features of unknown corpses for purposes of identification. This function was later replaced by photography. In the cases of people whose faces were damaged by their death, it was common to take casts of their hands.

42. **Tubes and Mirrors** - There were even coffins set up with tubes and mirrors so that gravediggers could peer into the coffin and look for movement.

Making of a death mask

SOME VICTORIAN FUNERAL SUPERSTITIONS

1. If the deceased has lived a good life, flowers would bloom on his grave; but if he has been evil, only weeds would grow.

2. If several deaths occur in the same family, tie a black ribbon to everything left alive that enters the house, even dogs and chickens. This will protect against deaths spreading further.

3. Never wear anything new to a funeral, especially shoes.

4. You should always cover your mouth while yawning so your spirit doesn't leave you and the devil never enters your body.

5. It is bad luck to meet a funeral procession head on. If you see one approaching, turn around. If this is unavoidable, hold on to a button until the funeral cortege passes.

6. Large drops of rain warn that there has just been a death.

7. Stop the clock in a death room or you will have bad luck.

8. To lock the door of your home after a funeral procession has left the house is bad luck.

9. If rain falls on a funeral procession, the deceased will go to heaven.

10. If you hear a clap of thunder following a burial it indicates that the soul of the departed has reached heaven.

11. If you hear 3 knocks and no one is there, it usually means someone close to you has died. The superstitious call this the 3 knocks of death.

12. If you leave something that belongs to you to the deceased, that means the person will come back to get you.

13. If a firefly/lightning bug gets into your house someone will soon die.

14. If you smell roses when none are around someone is going to die.

15. If you don't hold your breath while going by a graveyard you will not be buried.

16. If you see yourself in a dream, your death will follow.

17. If you see an owl in the daytime, there will be a death.

18. If you dream about a birth, someone you know will die.

19. If it rains in an open grave then someone in the family will die within the year.

20. If a bird pecks on your window or crashes into one that there has been a death.

21. If a sparrow lands on a piano, someone in the home will die.

22. If a picture falls off the wall, there will be a death of someone you know.

23. If you spill salt, throw a pinch of the spilt salt over your shoulder to prevent death.

24. Never speak ill of the dead because they will come back to haunt you or you will suffer misfortune.

25. Two deaths in the family means that a third is sure to follow.

26. The cry of a curlew or the hoot of an owl foretells a death.

27. A single snowdrop growing in the garden foretells a death.

28. Having only red and white flowers together in a vase (especially in hospital) means a death will soon follow.

29. Dropping an umbrella on the floor or opening one in the house means that there will be a murder in the house.

30. A diamond-shaped fold in clean linen portends death.

31. A dog howling at night when someone in the house is sick is a bad omen. It can be reversed by reaching under the bed and turning over a shoe.

Childhood Stuff

1. **COMIC BOOKS** - Reading and collecting comic books

2. **SLINKY**

3. **LIGHTENING BUGS** - Catching lightening bugs in a jar

4. **SPIN THE BOTTLE**

5. **PAPER CUTOUT DOLLS**

6. **RUBBER BAND GUNS** – zip guns

7. **BASEBALL CARDS IN THE SPOKES** of your bike to hear them pop (sounded like a machine gun)

8. **ICE SKATING** - ice skating on any pond or lake, every winter. When the Red Ball went up, it meant it was safe to skate.

9. **FLAV-R-STRAWS** - were a form of drinking straw with a flavoring included, designed to make drinking milk more pleasant for children. They were first marketed in the United States in 1956 by Flav-R-Straws Inc. The product became highly successful.

Strange Traditions

Most of these traditions are now a part of history (and in most cases that is a good thing) and most are considered barbaric or evil. Yet some of them have only stopped recently. This is the list of the top 10 bizarre traditions that are now mostly lost to mankind.

1. **GEISHA** - The full traditions of the Geisha have now been replaced with a modern system. Once Geisha were plentiful in number. In 1900s, there were over 25,000 geisha. In the early 1930s,

there were 80,000 geisha. Most geisha were in Kyoto, the old capital city of Japan. Nowadays, there are less than 10,000 geisha left. In Tokyo, there are only 100 geisha left. However, true geisha are much more rare. Modern geisha are not bought from poor families and brought into the geisha house as children. Becoming a geisha is now entirely voluntary, and women who are not the children of geisha can now become geisha. However the training remains as rigorous as before. Young girls have to be very committed to learn the art of traditional Japanese dancing, singing, music, and much more.
Traditional Geisha did not offer the services of prostitution, though some modern ones are rumored to.

2. **DUELING** - As practiced from the 15th to 20th centuries in Western societies, a duel was a consensual fight between two people, with matched deadly weapons, in accordance with rules explicitly or implicitly agreed upon, over a point of honor, usually accompanied by a trusted representative (who might themselves fight), and in contravention of the law.
The duel usually developed out of the desire of one party (the challenger) to redress a perceived insult to his honor. The goal of the duel was not so much to kill the opponent as to gain "satisfaction," to restore one's honor by showing a willingness to risk one's life for it.

Duels could be fought with some sort of sword or, from the 18th Century on, with pistols. For this end, special sets of dueling pistols were crafted for the wealthiest of noblemen. After the offense, whether real or imagined, the offended party would demand "satisfaction" from the offender, signaling this demand with an inescapably insulting gesture, such as throwing the glove before him, hence the phrase "throwing down the gauntlet".

3. **EUNUCHS** - A eunuch is a castrated man; the term usually refers to those castrated in order to perform a specific social function, as was common in many societies of the past. In ancient China castration was both a traditional punishment (until the Sui Dynasty) and a means of gaining employment in the Imperial service. At the end of the Ming Dynasty there were 70,000 eunuchs in the Imperial palace. The value of such employment—certain eunuchs gained immense power that may have superseded that of the prime ministers—was such that self-castration had to be made illegal. The number of eunuchs in Imperial employ had fallen to 470 in 1912, when their employment ceased Eunuchs castrated before puberty were also valued and trained in several cultures for their exceptional voices, which retained a childlike

and other-worldly flexibility and treble pitch. Such eunuchs were known as castrati. Unfortunately the choice had to be made at an age when the boy would not yet be able to consciously choose whether to sacrifice his sexual potency, and there was no guarantee that the voice would remain of musical excellence after the operation.

4. **CONCUBINAGE** - Concubinage is the state of a woman or youth in an ongoing, quasi-matrimonial relationship with a man of higher social status. Typically, the man has an official wife in addition to one or more concubines. Concubines have limited rights of support from the man, and their offspring are publicly acknowledged as the man's children, albeit of lower status than children born by the official wife or wives.
Historically, concubinage was frequently voluntary (by the girl and/or her family's arrangement), as it provided a measure of economic security for the woman involved. Involuntary, or servile, concubinage sometimes involves sexual slavery of one member of the relationship, typically the woman.

5. **SEPPUKU** - (Hara-Kiri) was a key part of
   Bushido, the code of the samurai warriors; it was
   used by warriors to avoid falling into enemy
   hands, and to attenuate shame. Samurai could
   also be ordered by their daimyo (feudal lords) to
   commit seppuku. Later, disgraced warriors were
   sometimes allowed to commit seppuku rather
   than be executed in the normal manner. Since
   the main point of the act was to restore or protect
   one's honor as a warrior, those who did not
   belong to the samurai caste were never ordered
   or expected to commit seppuku. Samurai women
   could only commit the act with permission.
   A Samurai was bathed, dressed in white robes,
   fed his favorite meal, and when he was finished,

his instrument was placed on his plate. Dressed ceremonially, with his sword placed in front of him and sometimes seated on special cloths, the warrior would prepare for death by writing a death poem. With his selected attendant (kaishakunin, his second) standing by, he would open his kimono (clothing), take up his tant (knife) and plunge it into his abdomen, making a left-to-right cut. The kaishakunin would then perform daki-kubi, a cut in which the warrior was all but decapitated (a slight band of flesh is left attaching the head to the body).

6. **HUMAN SACRIFICE** - Human sacrifice is the act of killing a human being for the purposes of making an offering to a deity or other, normally supernatural, power. It was practiced in many ancient cultures. The practice has varied between different cultures, with some like the Mayans and Aztecs being notorious for their ritual killings, while others have looked down on the practice as primitive. Victims were ritually killed in a manner that was supposed to please or appease gods or spirits. Victims ranged from prisoners to infants to Vestal Virgins, who suffered such fates as burning, beheading and being buried alive.
Over time human sacrifice has become less common around the world, and sacrifices are now very rare. Most religions condemn the practice and present-day laws generally treat it

as a criminal matter. Nonetheless it is still occasionally seen today, especially in the least developed areas of the world where traditional beliefs persist.

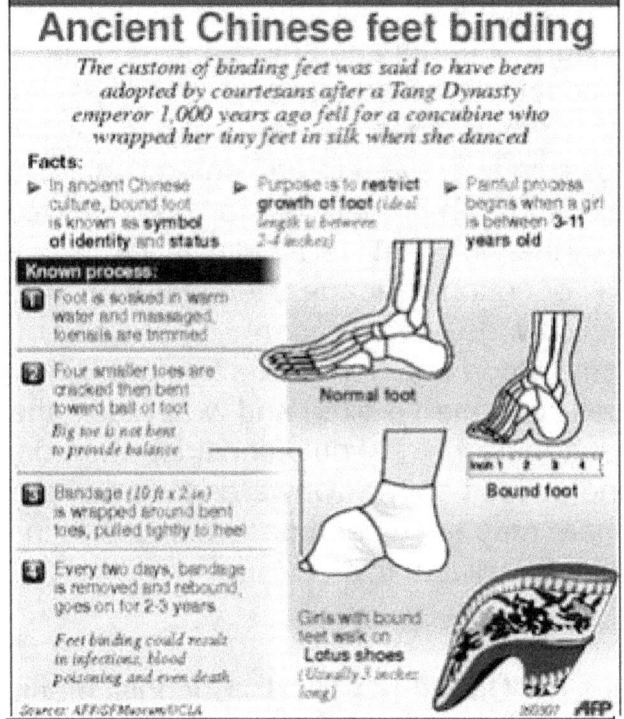

7. **FOOT BINDING** - Foot binding was a custom practiced on young females for approximately one thousand years in China, beginning in the 10th century and ending in the early 20th century. In Chinese foot binding, young girls'

feet, usually at age 6 but often earlier, were wrapped in tight bandages so that they could not grow and develop normally; they would, instead, break and become highly deformed, not growing past 4-6 inches (10-15 cm). Today, it is a prominent cause of disability among some elderly Chinese women.

First, each foot would be soaked in a warm mixture of herbs and animal blood. This concoction caused any necrotised flesh to fall off. Then her toenails were cut back as far as possible to prevent in-growth and subsequent infections. To prepare her for what was to come next the girl's feet were delicately massaged. Silk or cotton bandages, ten feet long and two inches wide, were prepared by soaking in the same blood and herb mix as before. Each of the toes were then broken and wrapped in the wet bandages, which would constrict when drying, and pulled tightly downwards toward the heel. There may have been deep cuts made in the sole to facilitate this.

8. **SELF-MUMMIFICATION** - Buddhist monks or priests who allegedly caused their own deaths in a way that resulted in their being mummified. This practice reportedly took place almost exclusively in northern Japan around the Yamagata Prefecture. Between 16 and 24 such mummifications have been discovered.

For three years the priests would eat a special diet consisting only of nuts and seeds, while taking part in a regimen of rigorous physical activity that stripped them of their body fat. They then ate only bark and roots for another three years and began drinking a poisonous tea made from the sap of the Urushi tree, normally used to lacquer bowls. This caused vomiting and a rapid loss of bodily fluids, and most importantly, it killed off any maggots that might cause the body to decay after death. Finally, a self-mummifying monk would lock himself in a stone tomb barely larger than his body, where he would not move from the lotus position. His only connection to the outside world was an air tube and a bell. Each day he rang a bell to let those outside know that he was still alive. When the bell stopped ringing, the tube was removed and the tomb sealed.

9. **TIBETAN SKY BURIAL** - Sky burial or ritual dissection was once a common practice in Tibet. A human corpse is cut into small pieces and placed on a mountaintop, exposing it to the elements and animals – especially to birds of prey. In one account, the leading monk cut off the limbs and hacked the body to pieces, handing each part to his assistants, who used rocks to pound the flesh and bones together to a pulp, which they mixed with tsampa (barley flour with tea and yak butter or milk) before the

vultures were summoned to eat.
In several accounts, the flesh was stripped from
the bones and given to vultures without further
preparation; the bones then were broken up with
sledgehammers, and usually mixed with tsampa
before being given to the vultures. In another
account, vultures were given the whole body.
When only the bones remained, they were
broken up with mallets, ground with tsampa, and
given to crows and hawks that had waited until
the vultures had departed.
The Communist government of China outlawed it
in the 1960's, so it was nearly a lost tradition, but
they legalized it again in the 1980s.

10. **SPITTING ON THE HAND** before shaking
hands. The Masai tribe, located in Kenya and
Tanzania, greeted each other by spitting. When
greeting elders, a tribesman would spit in his
hand before offering a handshake, thus showing
respect. The men spit on newborns, telling them
that they are bad. It is believed that if a baby is
praised, it will be cursed with a bad life.

11. **FINGER CUTTING** - While most cultures mourn
the loss of family members, women of the Dani
tribe in Indonesia must suffer great physical pain
in addition to emotional pain. When a family

member dies, female relatives must cut off a segment of one of their fingers. This practice is performed to satisfy ancestral ghosts. Luckily for the Dani women, this custom is rarely practiced anymore.

John Louis Sublett

Obsolete Occupations

In the 21st century, no one is surprised when automation and off-shoring render occupations obsolete. But that process of creative destruction has always occurred. Steel replaces bone. Siri the talking iPhone replaces Sally the switchboard operator. And as a result, we regard with wonder and puzzlement the lost jobs of our ancestors.

LECTOR

John Louis Sublett

The lector (or "reader") was a time-honored occupation that began in Cuba's cigar-making factories and then made its way to the United States throughout the 19th and early 20th centuries, particularly in Florida and New York. Workers pooled their wages to pay the lector to read to them. On a given day, the lector might read anything: Spanish-language newspapers, short stories, poems, novels, even English-language papers if his translation skills were sharp. Because lectors tended to be left-leaning and pro-labor, some were blamed by factory owners for their workers' unionist views. By the 1920s, many owners got rid of the lectors and replaced them with radios, but for decades, the lector was one of the most prestigious jobs among Latino factory workers.

ICEMAN

They delivered lake ice, 25 to 100-pound blocks of frozen water hacked from icebound lakes and rivers in New England and other northern climes, stored under sawdust in ice houses to stay cool, and delivered by the iceman in his horse-drawn cart to kitchens across America. That job finally melted away with the mass production of home refrigerators in the 1940's. After 1900, industrial refrigeration permitted the production of factory-produced ice. For the next 40 years, though, until home refrigerators became ubiquitous, families continued to display window signs telling icemen how many pounds of ice they needed delivered.

BARBER SURGEON - was one of the most common medical practitioners of medieval Europe – generally charged with looking after soldiers during or after a battle. In this era, surgery was not generally conducted by physicians, but by barbers. In the Middle Ages in Europe barbers would be expected to do anything from cutting hair to amputating limbs. Mortality of surgery at the time was quite high due to loss of blood and infection. Doctors of the Middle Ages thought that taking blood would help cure the patient of sickness so the barber would apply leeches to the patient. Physicians tended to be academics, working in universities, and mostly dealt with patients as an observer or a consultant. They considered surgery to be beneath them.

BARBER SURGEON

BABY FARMING - was a term used in late-Victorian Era Britain (and, less commonly, in Australia and the United States) to mean the taking in of an infant or child for payment; if the infant was young, this usually included wet-nursing (breast-feeding by a woman not the mother). Some baby farmers "adopted" children for lump-sum payments, while others cared for infants for periodic payments. Though baby farmers were paid in the understanding that care would be provided, the term "baby farmer" was used as an insult, and improper treatment was usually implied. Illegitimacy and its attendant stigma were usually the impetus for a mother's decision to put her children "out to nurse" with a baby farmer, but baby farming also encompassed foster care and adoption in the period before they were regulated by British law.

Richer women would also put their babies out to be cared for in the homes of villagers. Claire Tomalin gives a detailed account of this in her biography of Jane Austen, who was fostered in this manner, as were all her siblings, from a few months old until they were toddlers.

BOBBIN BOY - was a boy who worked in a textile mill in the 18th and early 19th centuries. He would bring bobbins to the women at the looms when they called for them, and collected the full bobbins of spun cotton or wool thread. They also would be expected to fix minor problems with the machines. Average pay was about $1.00 a week, with days often beginning at 5:30 am and ending around 7:30 pm six days a week. One example of rising from this job to great heights in America was young Andrew Carnegie, who at age 13 worked as a bobbin boy in 1848.[The job as a bobbin boy was extremely dangerous.

BOOK CANVASSERS

Door-to-door book peddlers of the 18th and 19th centuries, also known as "book canvassers", used to carry special "sample books", a kind of "preview", with table of contents, sample illustrations and some text, designed to advertise the book in question. Canvassing subscription sales were the only way to deliver books to many rural areas of America. Hawkers (peddlers) were often frowned upon by the law, but book peddlers were treated differently. For example, in laws of Massachusetts and Missouri that imposed penalties for hawkers operating without license, the book peddlers were excluded.

BREAKER BOY - was a coal-mining worker in the United States and United Kingdom whose job was to separate impurities from coal by hand in a coal breaker. Although breaker boys were primarily children, elderly coal miners who could no longer work in the mines because of age, disease, or accident were also sometimes employed as breaker boys. The use of breaker boys began in the mid-1860s. Although public disapproval of the employment of children as breaker boys existed by the mid-1880s, the practice did not end until the 1920s.

CABIN BOY - or ship's boy is a boy (in the sense of low-ranking male employee, not always a minor) who waits on the officers and passengers of a ship,especially running errands for the captain.

Cabin boys were usually 14–16 years old and also helped the cook in the galley and carried buckets of food from the galley to the forecastle where the ordinary seamen ate. They would have to run from one end of the ship to the other carrying messages and become familiar with the sails, lines and ropes and the use of each in all sorts of weather. They would have to scramble up the rigging into the yards whenever the sails had to be trimmed. They would even begin to stand watches like other crewmen or act as helmsman in good weather, holding the wheel to keep the ship steady on her course.

TURKEY DROVERS

It turns out that wild turkeys are incredibly difficult to move across long distances. In the days before refrigerated travel, a national roadway system, and even railroads, driving turkeys across long stretches of land was the province of men called turkey drovers. From 1790 to about 1830, turkey drovers walked turkeys to market, literally, at a top speed of about one mile per hour. Each fall during the nation's first decades, turkey drovers could be seen driving their turkeys across the lesser traveled byways of New England; the horse traffic of the day apparently proved a worthy distraction that slowed the driving of the turkeys even more. Turkey driving was a dawn-to-dusk activity. At the first sign of darkness, turkeys bolt for trees, ascend into them, and roost for the night. For this reason, turkey drovers, usually traveled in covered wagons and took turns protecting the roosting turkeys from predators (both animal fauna and humans) as well as from simply wandering off.

Another peril in turkey driving: turkeys tend to crowd together when being driven and will trample each other. To overcome this, men called shooers divided the turkeys into lots of up to 75 birds, and led the turkeys along their route using a long pole, with a piece of red flannel attached to the end.

TELEPHONE SWITCHBOARD OPERATOR

Long before dial tones and Siri, a person who wanted to make a call had to start the conversation with "Operator can you connect me…" and the person on the other end of the line was a switchboard operator. For decades the iconic image of the operator was of a row of poufy-haired 1930s women physically putting calls through to exchanges like "Murray Hill 5-9975." Later, people only needed an operator to make a collect call, but these days, while call centers exist, you're more likely to get an automated operator asking you to dial or say a number than an actual live person. For a real-life operator, you usually have to be experiencing an emergency.

LOG DRIVER

In the days before industrial trucking, log drivers transported cut trees from forests downriver to mills. Beginning with each year's spring thaw, these "river pigs" freed logs from sandbars, river rapids, and logjams. The men spent all day on water that was often near freezing, so to ease the cold and their own cracked skin, they greased their legs and waists with lard. The work was also dangerous. Bobbing logs made for unsteady work spaces, and a driver who fell through trunks faced a crushed limb or worse — if the trunks closed over him, he'd drown and his body might never resurface. For these risks, however, log drivers earned twice the pay of upriver lumberjacks ($2 versus $1 a day). The use of trucks in the 20th century allowed loggers to harvest trees without having to drive them downriver. That innovation, along with environmental laws, brought an end to this dangerous but lucrative business.

THEATER ORGAN PLAYER

The state-of-the-art theater sound was the theater organ. Organists accompanied silent movies played in grand theatrical palaces on equally grand pipe organs. Some keyboards could even play sound effects such as car horns, bird whistles, and ocean surf. By 1930, several thousand theaters had installed organs. But in 1927, the first talking picture, The Jazz Singer, premiered. As the Great Depression rolled around, theatergoers no longer wanted to hear, and theater owners no longer wanted to pay, theater organ players. As a result, many organists went on to accompany radio and early television shows on newly invented electric organs.

KNOCKER – UP (BEFORE ALARM CLOCKS)

Knocker-Up

Until the 1920s there was a profession called a knocker-up, which involved going from client to client and tapping on their windows (or banging on their doors) with long sticks until they woke up.

John Louis Sublett

BOWLING ALLEY PINSETTER (1910)

142

ICE CUTTER

Before modern refrigeration techniques became widespread, ice cutters would saw up the ice on frozen lakes for people to use in their cellars and refrigerators. It was a dangerous job often done in extreme conditions

PRE-RADAR LISTENER

Before radar, troops used acoustic mirrors and listening devices to focus and detect the sounds of engines from approaching enemy aircraft.

RAT CATCHER

Rat-catchers would capture rats by hand, often with specially-bred vermin terriers, or with traps. Rats are rarely seen in the open, preferring to hide in holes, haystacks and dark locations. Payment would be high for catching and selling rats to breeders. A rat-catcher's risk of being bitten is high, as is the risk of acquiring a disease from a rat bite.

LAMPLIGHTER

Leave it to the lamplighters to illuminate the darkened streets. Armed with a ladder and a light, these trusted workers would light each lamp at dusk, and return to extinguish them at dawn. Their job also included looking after the wicks and replenishing the fuel. With today's electric street lights, it's rare to see lamplighters anywhere in the world.

Lost Traditions

He made the night a little brighter
Wherever he would go
The old lamplighter
Of long, long ago
His snowy hair was so much whiter
Beneath the candle glow
The old lamplighter
Of long, long ago

You'd hear the patter of his feet
As he came toddling down the street
His smile would cheer a lonely heart you see
If there were sweethearts in the park
He'd pass a lamp and leave it dark
Remembering the days that used to be
For he recalled when things were new
He loved someone who loved him too
Who walks with him alone in memories

He made the night a little brighter
Wherever he would go
The old lamplighter

RESURRECTIONIST

Resurrectionists, or "body snatchers," were hired in the 19th century to remove corpses from graves for universities to use as cadavers. Cadavers from legal means were rare and difficult to obtain, so universities had to resort to other means to procure cadavers for their students.

CHIMNEY-SWEEPS

Someone who inspects and cleans chimneys. The job typically requires a certain level of dexterity since it involves a lot of climbing, squatting, kneeling, and stretching.

MILKMAN

Before everyone had refrigerators, milk quickly went bad. So you'd need it delivered regularly by your milkman. With home refrigeration, this profession disappeared

TOWN CRIER

Before radio, television and the internet, people relied on the town crier to deliver breaking news – in fact, town criers were used well into the 20th century in many parts of the US! While most of us now receive our news digitally, in the UK, town criers are still occasionally employed for special events.

ELEVATOR OPERATOR

Elevators were often controlled by a large lever which would cause the elevator to stop or run and sometimes also regulate speed, and typically required some skill or sense of timing to be able to consistently stop the elevator level with the doorway of a floor. Besides their training in operation and safety, later, department stores extended the roles of operators as combination greeters and tour guides, announcing product departments, floor-by-floor, and occasionally mentioning special price offers.

TYPESETTER

These days, there are endless graphic design-related computer programs. Before computers were the norm, however, typesetters were hired to manually lay text out onto paper. Most commonly, typesetters worked on print publications – in other words, every newspaper was laid out letter-by-letter. Tedious! Typesetters were still used up through the 1980's for things like advertising and package design.

TOLLBOOTH ATTENDANTS

They are already becoming an endangered species.
Now it's all about card-swiping, ez pass or coin
tossing.

Bizarre Dining Customs

These are now extinct

Water was not a table drink. Until relatively recently (think early 19th century), many municipal water supplies in the United States and most other Western countries were tainted. Many streets and rivers were little more than open sewers until the advent of underground plumbing, so water drawn from the nearest local water source was likely adulterated. The table drink of choice? Beer. The brewing process required boiling, so it was much more sanitary.

Salt was only for the rich. Salt was hard to come by and therefore expensive and highly prized. The most important item on a European dining table until about the 18th century was the "great salt," a large, ornate salt cellar that would act as the communal salt shaker for all at the table. These impressive objects now reside in museum collections around the world.

Savory ice cream. While chefs will always experiment with mixing sweet and savory, the Victorians took it to a new level. Ice cream was wildly popular in the late 19th century, and cookbook authors and newspaper columnists alike came up with all sorts of interesting recipes for it. While a "cucumber ice" actually sounds refreshing, a "salmon ice" does not. Lox in your ice cream? Yuck!

Official food taster. While this practice continues in some instances today — most notably at the 2008 Beijing Olympics when officials used white mice to test athletes' food — having a dedicated employee or servant to taste the food of an important ruler was common practice in ancient times. Though food tasters were popular, it's not certain whether they were actually effective, as most poisons are slow acting. The most notorious food taster was Halotus, who acted on behalf of Roman emperor Claudius. The emperor died of poisoning in AD 54, and his trusty food taster was implicated in the murder. So much for peace of mind!

Finger foods. Few of us can think of King Henry VIII without picturing him tearing into a chicken with his bare hands and with good reason. Forks are a relatively recent invention and weren't used at the table until well after the reign of Henry's daughter Elizabeth I. Until then, knives and spoons were used, and many men used the knives that they had sheathed at their waists.

Communal cups. Going along with the lack of forks, up until the English Restoration in 1660, only wealthy

Brits could afford individual glasses for their guests. Everyone else had to share, and a servant would pass them the cup from a shelf in the dining room known as the "cup board."

Peeing at the table. In Georgian times, dinner was practically an all-day affair and could last up to five hours. Without the advantage of indoor plumbing, some upper-class hosts took it upon themselves to provide a variety of chamber pots on the sideboard of their dining room. François de la Rochefoucauld, the French social reformer who was exiled to England after the French Revolution, was bewildered by this "most indecent" practice.

No family dinners. Most children in upper-class and upper-middle-class families in 1800's America and Britain were fed separately from their parents. Nannies would be charged with most of the childcare duties, including mealtimes, and most children would be in bed by 8:00, the usual time their parents would begin a multicourse dinner. Most young'uns didn't eat with their parents until they were old enough to learn table manners.

"Secret's in the sauce" You'd probably be upset if you found out your canned beans or pickles had sawdust or metal shavings in them. Unfortunately, adulterating food for mass consumption was common practice in the late 19th century, as exposed by Upton Sinclair in The Jungle. In the United States, the Pure Food and Drug Act of 1906 was one of the first official measures to combat this practice. It's also the reason H.J. Heinz sold his ketchup in glass bottles — the consumer could see for herself that there were no foreign objects inside.

Less-than-appetizing garnish. Native Americans may have been the experts at using all of an animal, but the Victorians turned it into an art. It was popular to serve exotic game with its head, wings or tail feathers as decoration. Anyone for a slice of stuffed peacock?

Our Ancestors

They wrote and received letters regularly

A hundred years from now, historians probably won't have nearly as much fun going through our old emails, and that's if someone has maintained the technology used to send them. Written correspondence — and the occasional telegram — was the only way most people could keep in touch with one another, and mail was delivered six times a day in some cities.

They got by without electricity

Turn off the power for 24 hours today and you'd get mass panic. We rely on electricity for everything from telephone communication to door locks to transportation. Most folks in the 1870s and '80s relied on candles, oil lamps, or built-in gas lighting for illumination, and they could cook, clean, and get around without all those volts. Once it was dark out, there was no reading under the covers — beddy bye!

They made their own household goods

Great-great-grandma probably sewed all her own household linens, complete with fancy embroidery, tatting, or other decorative embellishments. She could probably knit, crochet, or hook rugs. While some of these skills are becoming popular again, the ready availability of manufactured textiles has made most of them hobbies rather than essential life skills.

What Was It Like to Live in 18th-Century England?

•There were two very different lifestyles in 18th-century England: that of the rich and that of the poor. With the Industrial Revolution, which started in the middle of the century, came new machinery that saved time and made some people very wealthy. The rich were getting richer and the poor, poorer.

•Many people were out of work because suddenly machines were doing their jobs.

•The population was growing wildly. Cities were dirty, noisy, and overcrowded. London had about 600,000 people around 1700 and almost a million residents in 1800.

•The rich, only a tiny minority of the population, lived luxuriously in lavish, elegant mansions and country houses, which they furnished with comfortable, upholstered furniture.

•Their calendars included dinner parties, opera, and the theater. Many had inherited their great fortunes and never knew what it was to have to work, cook meals, or empty their own chamber pots.

•Fashion was important in upper society: Upper-class women wore stays, which were bodices with strips of whalebone, and hooped petticoats under their dresses.

•Men wore knee-length "breeches" with stockings, waistcoats, and frock coats over linen shirts, as well as buckled shoes. Three-cornered hats were popular, so were wigs.

•Schools were not compulsory, but many upper-class boys attended school, and some girls from well-off families did, too. Girls were educated more in "accomplishments" like embroidery and music than in academic subjects.

•Some "charity schools" started to provide an education to lower-class children.

•Tea drinking became popular in the 1700s among both the rich and the poor.

•Poor people ate rather plain and monotonous diets made up primarily of bread and potatoes; meat was an uncommon luxury.

•Poor craftsmen and laborers lived in just two or three rooms, and the poorest families lived in just one room with very simple and plain furniture.

•It was a difficult life for poor people: There was no government assistance for the unemployed, and many had trouble finding their next meal or a warm place to sleep.

•For every 1,000 children born in early-18th-century London, almost 500 died before they were 2, generally due to malnutrition, bad water, dirty food, and poor hygiene.

•Orphans roamed the streets; because they didn't attend school, they had little chance of improving their situation.

Strange and Unusual Taxes

Throughout history there have been many strange, unusual, and weird taxes. Many of them were implemented to raise additional revenue, while the purpose of others was to promote social change. Here are some of the strangest ones:

• **COOKING OIL TAX** - In Ancient Egypt, cooking oil was taxed, and on top of that, people had to buy their taxed cooking oil from the Pharaoh's monopoly, and were prohibited from reusing previously purchased oil.

• **URINE TAX** - During the 1st century AD, Roman emperor Vaspasian placed a tax on urine. The buyer(s) of the urine paid the tax. Pecunia non olet or Money doesn't stink! is a Latin saying. During the 1st century AD, Roman emperor Vaspasian placed a tax on urine. The buyer(s) of the urine paid the tax. The urine from public urinals was sold as an essential ingredient for several chemical processes e.g. it was used in tanning (not exactly sure how), and also by launderers as a source of ammonia to clean and whiten woolen togas etc. Therefore, those who obtained valuable urine from collectors were charged a tax.

• **SLAVE TAX** - In Ancient Rome, it was not uncommon for slave owners to free their slaves after a certain number of years of work, and/or the payment of a certain fee. Slaves could pay that fee because many of them had the opportunity to work in several places, and thus could earn the money used to obtain their freedom. The Roman government required the newly freed slave to pay a tax on his or her freedom.

• **SOAP TAX** - During the Middle Ages, European governments placed a tax on soap. It remained in effect for a very long time. Great Britain didn't repeal its soap tax until 1835.

• **CHICKEN OUT TAX** - King Henry I allowed knights to opt out of their duties to fight in wars by paying a tax called "scutage". At first the tax wasn't high, but then King John came to power and raised it to a rate of 300%. Some claim that the excessive tax rate was one of the things that contributed to the creation of the Magna Carta, which limited the king's power.

• **PLAYING CARDS** - were taxed as early as the 16th century, but in 1710, the English government dramatically raised taxes on playing cards and dice. This led to widespread forgeries of playing cards to avoid paying taxes. The tax was not removed until 1960.

• **FIREPLACE TAX** - n 1660, England placed a tax on fireplaces. The tax led to people covering their fireplaces with bricks to conceal them and avoid paying the tax. It was repealed in 1689.

• **WINDOW TAX** - England implemented a window tax, taxing houses based on the number of windows they had. In 1696, England implemented a window tax, taxing houses based on the number of windows they had. That led to many houses having very few windows in order to avoid paying the tax. Eventually this became a health problem and ultimately led to the tax's repeal in 1851.

• **BRICK TAX** - In the 1700's, England placed a tax on bricks. Builders soon realized that they could use bigger bricks (and thus fewer bricks) to pay less tax. Soon after, the government caught on and placed a larger tax on bigger bricks. Brick taxes were finally repealed in 1850.

• **BEARD TAX** - In 1705, Russian Emperor Peter the Great placed a tax on beards, hoping to force men to adopt the clean-shaven look that was common in Western Europe.

• **SALT TAX** - The French had a salt tax called the gabelle, which angered many and was one of the contributing factors to the French Revolution.

• **WALLPAPER TAX** - England imposed a tax on printed wallpaper. Builders avoided the tax by hanging plain wallpaper and then painting patterns on the walls. In 1712, England imposed a tax on printed wallpaper. Builders avoided the tax by hanging plain wallpaper and then painting patterns on the walls.

• **TAX ON HATS** - England introduced a tax on hats in 1784. To avoid the tax, hat-makers stopped calling their creations "hats", leading to a tax on any headgear by 1804. The tax was repealed in 1811.

• **CANDLE TAX** - In 1789, England introduced a tax on candles. People were forbidden from making their own candles unless they obtained a license and then paid taxes on the candles they produced. The tax was repealed in 1831, leading to a more widespread popularity of candles.

• **CHINESE TAX** - In 1885 Canada created the Chinese Head Tax, which taxed the entry of Chinese immigrants into Canada. The tax lasted until 1923 when a law was passed banning Chinese people from entering Canada altogether with a few exceptions.

• **TELEVISION TAX** - England has a tax on televisions. If you own a television in your home, you must pay an annual fee, formally called a television license, for each television you own. This money is used to finance programming on the BBC. Color televisions are taxed at a higher rate than black and white televisions. Interestingly enough, if a person is blind an owns a TV in his or her home, he or she still has to pay the tax, but only half of it. Failure to pay this fee is subject to criminal penalties. There were 155,000 convictions and fines in 2012 alone.

• **BLUEBERRY TAX** - Maine has special tax on blueberries, a valuable state resource.

• **VACUUM TAX** - Pennsylvania has a tax on coin-operated vacuum machines at gas stations.

• **AMUSEMENT TAX** - Pittsburgh has a 5% amusement tax on anything that offers entertainment or allows people to engage in entertainment.

• **PUMPKIN TAX** - States like Iowa, Pennsylvania, and New Jersey exempt pumpkins from a sales tax but only if they will be eaten and not carved.

• **TAX ON DRUG DEALERS** - n 2005, Tennessee began requiring drug dealers to anonymously pay taxes on any illegal substances they sold.

• **MARIJUANA TAX** - Despite marijuana being illegal on a federal level and in most states, many states impose taxes on the sale of marijuana.

• **SNUFF TAX** - n California, snuff tobacco is taxed differently depending on its type. Dry snuff is taxed at 256% of its price if it's $1.70 or more. Moist snuff is taxed at 170% of its price if it's $1.70 or more.

• **CANDY TAX** - In Chicago, candy that is prepared with flour is taxed as food at 1%, while candy that is prepared without flour is taxed as candy at 6.25%.In Chicago, candy that is prepared with flour is taxed as food at 1%, while candy that is prepared without flour is taxed as candy at 6.25%.

• **CASINO TAX** - Numerous states charge a tax on admissions to racetracks and casinos.

• **FRUIT TAX** - In California, fresh fruit bought through a vending machine is subject to a 33% tax.

• **STUD FEE** - Kentucky levies a sales tax on thoroughbred stud fees (whether the horses were in the Derby or not).

• **TAX ON STOLEN PROPERTY** - The IRS taxes stolen property. The 1040 instructions say that you should report it as stolen property. However, doing that would be self-incrimination, from which we are protected by the Constitution; therefore, one has the option of reporting it as "other income".

• **CHRISTMAS TAX** - In Texas, Christmas tree decoration services are subject to a tax only if the decorator provides the decorations and ornaments. In addition, there is a tax on holiday-themed pictures that are meant to be placed on windows.

• **JOCK TAX** - Many cities and states levy a "jock tax" on any income earned by entertainers and athletes while working in that city. Many cities and states levy a "jock tax" on any income earned by entertainers and athletes while working in that city. Therefore, athletes have to pay taxes on a portion of their income in any place they play.

• **INTERNET TAX** - Wisconsin is one of the few states that levies a tax on internet access. When dial-up was a popular method of getting online, there was double taxation occurring because phone calls were also taxed.

• **SODA TAX** - The City of Chicago taxes soda bought in a bottle at a rate of 3%, and taxes soda from fountains at a rate of 9%.

• **LITIGATION TAX** - In Tennessee, there is a tax on all litigation. The amount varies case-by-case but it can be as low as $1 for a parking violation case. The tax tends to discourage frivolous lawsuits.

• **FUR TAX** - In Minnesota, there is a special tax on fur.

• **HOT AIR BALLOON TAX** - In the state of Kansas, untethered hot air balloon rides are exempt from sales tax because they are considered a legitimate form or air transportation. Tethered hot air balloon rides, on the other hand, are considered to be an amusement ride and therefore are subject to sales tax.

• **TAX ON NUDE SHOWS** - In 2007 Texas lawmakers imposed a $5 tax on establishments that host live nude shows and also allow alcohol consumption on their premises. Since strip clubs are the businesses that are affected by it, the tax was nicknamed the "pole tax". The revenue from the tax goes to help help sexual assault victims and provide health insurance for the poor. The tax was challenged in the Texas Supreme Court on First Amendment grounds, but was upheld in 2011.

• **OLYMPIC TAX** - In 2012 there was a controversy after the London Summer Olympic Games about the tax treatment of foreign athletes competing in Great Britain. According to the British tax code, foreign athletes competing in the UK have all their endorsement income taxed, even income originating from other countries, and the income is taxed proportionally to the time spent in the UK. This is different from the way many other countries, including the United States, tax foreign athletes. In the United States only endorsement income of foreign athletes originating from US sponsors is taxed by the IRS. The law was waived by the British government for the duration of the Olympic Games, but it kicked back in after the conclusion of the games. A number of high profile athletes have spoken out against this tax, stating that their tax bill may be bigger than any prize they may receive by winning the competition. The law is often cited by athletes as a reason for choosing to avoid attending competitions in Great Britain.

Obsolete

- **PUBLIC HANGING** - An obsolete custom I'd like to see revived is public hanging. Carried out within 7 days of a guilty verdict

- **PUBLICLY FLOGGING**

- **VHS TAPES** - In 2005, the Washington Post penned an obituary of sorts for the VHS tape, writing, "VHS -- the beloved videotape format that bravely won the war against Betamax and charmed millions of Americans by allowing them to enjoy mindless Hollywood entertainment without leaving their homes -- has died at the age of 29. It passed away peacefully after a long illness caused by chronic technological insignificance and a lack of director's commentary tracks." The president of the Video Software Dealers Association told the Post he thought 2006 would be "the last year that there are major releases on VHS, and there won't be many of those."

- **WIRES** - Wireless internet, wireless updating, wireless downloads, wireless charging, wireless headphones: Although wires are still around (for now!), they're well on their way to being a thing of the past.

- **HAND-WRITTEN LETTERS** - Love letters, thank you notes, and invitations have gone being hand-written to typed, and from the mailbox to the inbox. Sending online messages is a bargain next to $.44 stamp.

- **LICKABLE STAMPS** - Collectors still like them, but the rest of us want self-adhesives.

- **INCANDESCENT LIGHT BULB** - The curly light bulbs are trying to replace these, but haven't quite made it ... yet

- **LASER DISCS** - Let's be fair: These never really caught on in the first place.

- **CASH** - Who needs it anymore when you can pay for everything with a credit or debit card? It has become just dirty paper that is way too easy to lose or have taken from you.

- **PRINT PHOTOS**

- **TV GUIDES**

- **MANUAL CAR WINDOWS**

- **ROLODEXES**

- **CHECKS**

- **CARBON COPIES**

- **HOTEL KEYS**

- **ANSWERING MACHINE**

- **OLD CINEMA TRADITION OF CARTOONS AND A NEWSREEL**

- **SING ALONG FOLLOWING THE BOUNCING BALL**

- **GETTING FILM DEVELOPED**

- **8 TRACK TAPES**

- **LASER DISCS**

- **FOUNTAIN PENS**

- **TYPEWRITER**

- **FOLDING MAPS**

- **PUBLIC PAY PHONES**

- **PAID EMAIL ACCOUNTS**

- **NEWSPAPER CLASSIFIEDS**

- **PHONE BOOKS**

- **CALLING 411**

- **BILLS IN THE MAIL**

- **RECORD STORES**

John Louis Sublett

- **BOOKSTORES**

- **WATCHES**

- **CATALOGS**

- **CAMERAS**

- **SLIDE PROJECTORS**

- **WHITE OUT**

- **AUTOMATS**

Soon to be Obsolete

- **HOME PHONES** - With wireless penetration in the U.S. currently at 102.2%, it's no surprise that many people are using their mobiles or internet voice services as their primary way to connect. And when we consider the fact that about one-fifth of American households were wireless-only as of June 2009, it's not hard to conclude that the landline is on its way out.

- **PUBLIC PAY PHONES** - Even homeless people have cell phones now. Though, New York City is trying to reinvent its payphones and find alternate uses for them.

- **FILM DEVELOPING** and printing.

- **MOVIE RENTAL STORES** - The massive popularity of Netflix and Video-On-Demand has made it virtually unnecessary to go to an actual store to rent movies. Blockbuster is feeling the shift.

- **PHYSICAL MAPS** - No more getting lost on those epic road trips or in the woods (unless you lose cell service)... just punch in your destination into your GPS or smartphone and you're good to go.

- **VCR's** - DVD players first outsold VCR's in 2002; by 2004, they were outselling them at 40 to 1.

Combine that total shift to digital movie-watching with the development of DVR, and you had the inevitable death of the poor VCR.

- **PHONE BOOKS** – you can look up any number online

- **DICTIONARIES, ENCYCLOPEDIAS** - Our old bastions of data have been fading fast over the last few years, replaced by -- what else?-- the Internet.

- **NEWSPAPERS** - Probably the biggest casualty of the decade. With most communication now conducted online, magazines and newspapers crumbling, and e-readers increasing in popularity, newspapers are now on serious life support.

- **COMPACT DISCS** - Poor CD's. But could anything really have withstood the amazing convenience of digital music and the worldwide adoption of the iPod? As CD sales dropped by 15% this year, it's only a matter of time until the CD becomes just a relic of times bygone.

- **RECORD STORES** - Records have long been obsolete, except as nostalgia. But the record store, as in a store that sells music, has now been replaced by the internet and iTunes.

Obsolete Disease

Vaccines are considered by many to be the most successful medical discovery of all time. Many diseases that killed people by the millions are now all but wiped out. Diseases that have been virtually eliminated by modern vaccines include:

• **SMALLPOX**: Even as late as the 1950s, smallpox was infecting as many as 50 million people a year worldwide [source: WHO]. If it didn't kill you, smallpox could scar you for life or even leave you blind.

• **POLIO**: As late as the 1950s, more than 20,000 cases of polio were reported in the U.S. each year, resulting in paralysis or even death. Less than 20 years after a vaccine became available, polio infections were reduced to about 10 total [source: CDC Polio].

• **MEASLES**: As recently as about 1991, there were 120 deaths from measles in the United States. The disease was practically wiped out in the United States, along with rubella, thanks to the 1971 licensing of the measles, mumps and rubella vaccine [source: CDC]. In the first half of 2011, however, there were 156 confirmed cases of measles; these most likely occurred among people who had not been vaccinated and traveled abroad [source: Health Advisory].

• **DIPHTHERIA**: Diphtheria is usually a disease of the throat and nose and is caused by bacteria. Diphtheria is spread through the shared use of personal items and airborne droplets. A vaccine to treat diphtheria was developed in 1913 and has led to a significant drop in mortality rates. However, in parts of the world where people aren't vaccinated on a regular basis, diphtheria still exist. According to the World Health Organization, approximately 5,000 people worldwide die every year from diphtheria. In the U.S., diphtheria has been virtually eradicated, with no more than five deaths per year being attributed to it.

www.ingramcontent.com/pod-product-compliance
Lightning Source LLC
Chambersburg PA
CBHW071042290526
45795CB00004B/1273

* 9 7 8 1 4 9 3 7 8 2 1 5 4 *